ALL THINGS NEW

The Promise of Advent, Christmas and the New Year

by
Gerald O'Collins, S.J.

PAULIST PRESS
New York/ Mahwah, N.J.

Cover design by Frank Vitale

Library of Congress Cataloging-in-Publication Data

O'Collins, Gerald.
    All things new : the promise of Advent, Christmas, and the New Year
/ by Gerald O'Collins.
        p.   cm.
    Includes index.
    ISBN 0-8091-3824-7 (alk. paper)
        1. Advent. 2. Christmas. 3. New Year. I. Title.
BV40.033   1998
242'.33—dc21   98–17579
                                                                    CIP

Published by Paulist Press
997 Macarthur Boulevard
Mahwah, New Jersey 07430

Printed and bound in the
United States of America

CONTENTS

THE NEW YEAR

Introduction

Inevitably, as the second Christian millennium draws to a close and we slip into the third millennium, Advent, Christmas and the New Year seem more precious than ever. The fresh sensitivity to time that the change of millennia triggers can make us more spiritually alert as we move through December into January. Before I came to live and work in Italy twenty-five years ago, Christmas and the New Year meant a great deal to me. Then, life in Rome at the Gregorian University taught me to appreciate Advent more deeply. The Advent carol services around the city, the wreaths with four purple candles burning down one after the other, customs connected with the feast of St. Nicholas (6 December) and of Mary's Immaculate Conception (8 December) and other practices all played a role in moving me into and through the four weeks of Advent.

This new appreciation of Advent has often called to mind a text I used to hear long ago from the great German theologian, Jürgen Moltmann: "Do not remember the former things, or consider the things of old. I am about to do a new thing" (Is 43:18–19). God announces here the return to Palestine from the Babylonian captivity, a deliverance that will be even more astonishing than the original deliverance from Egypt. This is a very suggestive text about Advent, not only for the church community at large but also for each of us as individuals.

No Advent is or should be like any other Advent. Our spiritual life and experience of God are never meant to be a mere repetition of what has gone before. God is not saying to us: "Remember the former Advents and consider the Advents of old. Behold, I am doing the same old thing for you." Rather, God is saying to us: "Remember not the former Advents nor consider the Advents of old. Behold, I am doing a new thing this Advent." More than ever, now at the change of millennia, God promises to make all things new for everyone: O'Collins, Boadt, Brophy, Costacurta, Longford, Lynch, Trench, Wicks and the lot of us. The temptation against which our Isaiah text should put us on guard is that of drifting into thinking: "O'Collins, yesterday, today and the same forever; as he was in the beginning, is now and ever shall be, faults without end. Amen." God is rather in the business of making new persons of us. No Advent, Christmas and New Year should be like any other Advent, Christmas and New Year. For the community at large and for us as individuals, the divine guarantee comes through clearly: "I am doing a new thing. I am making all things new."

Introduction

In this book I want to think about what God offers us in Jesus, through the Holy Spirit and through life with one another. If what I write helps readers to experience Advent, Christmas and the New Year more vividly and powerfully, I will be more than satisfied. My special thanks go to Philip Rosato, S.J., for various improvements and corrections to the text. I dedicate this book to Jared Wicks, S.J., the best of friends and one to whom I owe a very great debt of gratitude.

Gregorian University, Rome.
20 December 1997.
Gerald O'Collins, S.J.

ADVENT

Chapter One:
The Advent God: "Time, Gentlemen, Please!"

Many years ago a friend of mine was studying the works of T. S. Eliot. In *The Waste Land* he came across the phrase "Hurry please it's time." My friend, who had thus far led a quiet and cloistered life, puzzled over the meaning of the words. Eventually he thought he could see what the phrase meant, but decided to check what even the charitable had to call an embarrassingly far-fetched interpretation with the author himself. So he wrote to Eliot, asking whether his interpretation corresponded to what the poet had intended. Eliot responded fairly soon and said: "Well, those words *could* mean what you suggest. But all I had in mind was what the owner says in an English pub when it comes toward closing time. The pub owner says: 'Time, gentlemen, please!' Everyone drinks up and leaves the pub. Then the owner can lock up for the night."

Toward the end of November we can be more conscious of time running out on us than at any other period in the year. In less than no time Christmas and the New Year will be upon us; the year is closing down. Perhaps we are counting the days until that happens, maybe even crossing off one day after another until the last day of the year actually arrives. December and the end of the current year can make us think a great deal about time.

What is time? How do we experience it? Perhaps as an enemy. "I am terribly pressed for time. I have no time to spend with my family and friends. My business keeps me too busy to pray, read the Bible and spend time with God. There is so much that I would love to do with others and for others, but my job never leaves me with a free moment." Time can seem like a cruel enemy, or at least a demanding master who stops us from doing the things we would love to do.

Or maybe we think of time as the space which we control and fill up with our work. I use time to do things: to get to the office, to meet some clients, attend to some appointments, finish a paper for my boss, take my children to a film, visit my sick aunt. I plan things carefully and make the best of time, and use it to my advantage and to the advantage of those I am responsible for.

The season of Advent offers us an alternate view of time. Instead of being an enemy on the scene of my careful planning and efficient activity, time involves the coming to us of our loving God. In December God comes to us—through the wilderness and desert of our lives and our world. The kingdom of God is at hand; a new day is dawning; and our infinitely caring God draws near to us.

Advent encourages us to "locate" God in the future. In the Book of Revelation we read: "'I am the Alpha and the Omega,' says the Lord God, who is and who was and who *is to come*" (Rv 1:8). God is not described here as we might expect, as the One who is and who was and who will be—that is to say, as equally related to past, present and future. Revelation highlights the coming God, the God of the future.

"Locating" God in the future means respecting the divine initiative that goes beyond anything we can plan and manipulate. Taught by experience, we know that what will in fact happen consistently outstrips our predictions. The future introduces the element of the unmanageable and the unpredictable. There is no key to the present situation that would infallibly reveal how the future must evolve. In acknowledging the "futurity" of our Advent God, we are acknowledging the divine creativity and freedom that elude and transcend all human control.

In this connection Rudolf Otto's classic account of the Holy as the *mysterium tremendum et fascinans* (the frightening and fascinating mystery) enjoys a fresh application. God is the unpredictable mystery of the future that is both terrifying and enthralling. The future engages and attracts us with the seemingly unlimited possibilities it holds out. It is at the same time fearful because it is unknown and in many ways uncontrollable. God is this numinous power of the future, the One who will not be fully our God until the final kingdom comes.

So far I have lived a quarter of a century in Italy, after first arriving to teach part-time at the Gregorian University in 1973 and full-time a year later. Italians and their country have blessed me in so many ways, and not least with their enchanting language. One of its advantages consists in having (like German and some other languages) two words for the future: *futuro* and *avvenire*. Where *futuro* and, for that matter, our English word *future* can too readily suggest something growing out of the present, *avvenire* like *Ad-vent* points to the arrival or "coming to us" of something or, better, of Someone who is approaching us. *Avvenire* and *Advent* create a sense of expectancy. This season is bringing God near to us. God is coming to enlighten and redeem us.

Over the years one of the most moving sermons I have heard in Rome was preached by George Carey, the Archbishop of Canterbury, when he was spending several days visiting Pope John Paul II and some Vatican officials. As his visit coincided with the start of Advent, the Archbishop developed his thoughts out of a classical distinction between two Greek words: *Chronos,* or the time that we measure and live by, and *Kairos,* or the favorable time or blessed opportunity. *Chronos* is the time which at best we control and which at worst robs us of all kinds of people and possibilities. "Devouring time" eats up so much that we value, love and enjoy. But, as Dr. Carey insisted in the Advent context, time is far from being something that we "make" or "take," let alone something that devours us. Advent time is truly a *kairos,* a gift held out to us by the God who comes to heal and save us.

December is the closing time of the calendar year, a month of changes measured by clocks when various people say to us: "Time, gentlemen, please!" But, unlike an English pub on a winter's evening, Advent is not the time to drink up and go out in the cold night. Rather the Advent *kairos* invites us to stay inside and wait in the warm light. We do not have to leave. God is coming to us and wants to heal our wounds, save our lives, and fill us with the never-ending joy of Jesus' presence.

One might boldly imagine God as the most wonderful pub owner who says to all of us: "It's time, ladies and gentlemen, please—time to appreciate how your earthly existence is tied to my eternity. Hurry, please, because it's time to accept my love, my light and my warmth."

Chapter Two:
St. Mark, the Voice Crying in the Wilderness

All four gospels offer special help for our journey through Advent to Christmas and the New Year. Not least St. Mark's gospel, with its opening message of repentance being preached in the desert as the kingdom of God is coming fast (Mk 1:1–15). Place, time and a sense of mystery join in creating a serious, even a life-and-death atmosphere.

We should not miss the place and timing of this message of repentance and forgiveness: its geography and history, if you like. The place is the desert, and the time is the grace-filled moment of the divine kingdom breaking into our world. Always and everywhere space and time shape the way we perceive and respond to reality, and not least in Advent when we respond to the reality of God and ourselves.

The divine message comes to people in a special place, the desert. This is a privileged setting for God to encounter us—out in the desert, far from towns and cities, away from our homes and other places filled by human beings, their products, their noise and their busy activities. God can get at us in the desert. It is a favored space where God and the divine message come to bear on us. It is also the setting where we can let ourselves be opened to hear that message and respond to the divine reality.

Years ago, in a kind of "Easy Rider" mood, I drove with two friends across the United States from California to Massachusetts. Leaving Los Angeles at noon, we made our first stop at Las Vegas. My imagination rebelled when we left the awesome beauty of the desert for the tawdry glitter and compulsive gambling of Caesar's Palace. We seemed to have left God behind along the road and to have arrived at the gaudy and even hellish nonsense of a casino city. But once I began meeting people there, I came to realize how even the garish frivolity of Las Vegas can turn into a fruitful wilderness, a place where the human spirit may find itself alone with God.

At the beginning of Mark's gospel, the wilderness creates a fruitful geography, and the historical timing is also quite right. John proclaims to sinners a "baptism of repentance," and Jesus will announce: "the kingdom of God has come near." God's rule and reign are breaking into our history. Time is short; the future is bearing down on us. God is approaching and approaching us fast. Mark's opening verses convey a pressing sense of urgency about the way we should respond. In the message of John the Baptist, space and time conspire to underline the pressing emergency his hearers are facing. "Out here in the desert you cannot get away from God. You have very little time left, for God is coming to confront you."

This message clamors for our attention as the current year is running out for us. Christmas and the coming of Christ are at hand. The nineties are ending, and the third millennium is at hand. In this Advent we find ourselves in the right place and the right time to let the course of our lives be deeply changed. This is God's place and God's time. There can be no better place and time for being made ready to welcome the coming of the Lord.

But who is this God so concerned about all of us? Mark's gospel begins by offering the hint of an answer. God is the One who takes a mysterious initiative: "See, I am sending my messenger." The divine initiative is not yet clearly defined. Something is about to happen; in some way God has set in train a new series of events, and is moving to meet us. "Prepare the way of the Lord." God is approaching us and will be revealed to us. Through Jesus we will be able to know at least something of the ultimate mystery of God.

Not much is said. But the opening of Mark's gospel creates an air of expectancy. Divine preparations are on the way. We are invited to open ourselves to the mysterious initiatives of God, even if thus far we can grasp very little of who God is and what God is about. More than in any other season of the year, God calls on us in Advent to open and abandon ourselves to the mystery about to unfold before our eyes.

Chapter Three:
St. Matthew, Our Guide for Advent

Many years ago a teacher of mine in England received an invitation to lead a day of prayer for a group of people. Initially they were dismayed when he took as his text Matthew 1:1–17, the elaborate genealogy of Jesus that opens the collection of New Testament books. The family tree begins with Abraham and Sarah, moves on through fourteen generations to King David, then traces another fourteen generations to the exile in Babylon and ends with fourteen generations down to Jesus himself. Older translations sounded comic with their "begats" and "begots." In any case, while it was not too hard to say "Abraham begot Isaac," some of the subsequent names such as "Aminadab," "Rehoboam," and "Zerubbabel" could prove to be awkward, even comic, tongue twisters. My friend used these apparently unpromising verses to develop a central theme for reflection and prayer: all human history is in the divine hands. Despite human weakness and wickedness, "all shall be well, and all manner of thing shall be well." God will write straight even if we provide some rather crooked lines.

And there are some pretty crooked lines in Matthew's list of Jesus' forebears. David, for example, committed adultery and murder on the way to acquiring Bathsheba as his wife and the mother of his successor, Solomon (2 Sm 11:2–12:24). We are dealing here with an absolutely key figure in this family tree. King David provided Jesus with royal lineage. That made him essential for Matthew's three groups of fourteen names; fourteen is the sum of the numerical value of the three letters in the name "David" in Hebrew (DWD). David confessed: "I have sinned against the Lord" (2 Sm 12:13). But he also continued to trust that God would "write straight" by carrying through the promise to make David's dynasty everlasting (2 Sm 7:1–29). In and through Jesus, the Son of David par excellence, God did just that.

The device of introducing three groups of ancestors clearly helped people to remember the whole genealogy. But Matthew's device may also be seen as more than a mere aid for fallible human memory. It implies faith in the God who not only holds history together but also turns it into the supremely good news that is the coming of Jesus. History has a pattern *and* a face, and the face will be that of the tiny baby in the arms of Mary. In putting together and then looking back at their family tree, people normally disclose a sense of their own uniqueness. All these men and women who were my ancestors conspired to produce the one and only "me." Every genealogy implies a providential line that leads to the appearance of someone. Beyond question, all human beings are unique and part of God's good news, but Jesus is incomparably so. Matthew's genealogy provides the background for expressing faith in Jesus' utterly incomparable identity as "God with us" (Mt 1:23) and the One who "will save his people from their sins" (Mt 1:21).

Whenever I read Matthew's words about Jesus being "Emmanuel" or "God with us," I think of a friend who years ago complained to me about what he took to be the poor state of Roman Catholicism in France. His voice faltered and he summed things up: "The French went in for Catholic Action. Then they pushed the line of *témoignage* or witness. Now they are satisfied with mere presence." To be sure, we can make of "presence" something insignificant, a weak excuse for slothful detachment. But true personal presence is the very antithesis of that. Every day of our lives we look for the presence of those whom we care for and whose care for us makes us live and grow. We cannot endure to leave friendship and love at a distance. Photographs, memories, letters, faxes and even phone calls are not enough. We want to enjoy the personal presence of those who fill our minds and let us live in their hearts. We live in God's heart, and Matthew's name for Jesus reminds us that God did not want to live that love at a distance. Jesus is and gives us God's personal presence. This divine self-sharing and self-giving make God's love for us truly believable and powerfully effective. So far from being "the child of a lesser god," someone who will grow up and become commissioned by God as another prophet, Jesus is God-come-to-be-with-us, the Emmanuel who wants to be always and everywhere present to us. So long live French Catholics and their distinguished philosopher who spent years exploring the rich, life-giving qualities of presence, Gabriel Marcel (d. 1973). He showed us how genuine presence is truly the face of love. Matthew may not have been a philosopher, but he knew that as Emmanuel Jesus was and is the face of God's love present among us.

Over the years I have lectured in different parts of the world. In the question and answer period that followed the lecture I have always wanted the last question to reach the heart of the matter. This happened at least once—at St. Louis University after I had spoken on images and titles of Jesus. "Would you share with us your favorite title for Jesus?" the last questioner asked. "It has to be his name, 'Jesus'," I replied. "Of course," I added, "some or even many scholars think here simply of the name by which he was known in history. But it is a name with a rich message: it means 'God saves or God is salvation.' This personal name is very special and intimate; calling him by his name lets us feel how close he is. That, by the way, is the reason for the titles I chose for a number of my books: from *The Easter Jesus* in 1973, through *What Are They Saying About Jesus?, A Month with Jesus, Finding Jesus, Jesus Today* and *Jesus Risen,* right down to *Experiencing Jesus* in 1994 and *Focus on Jesus* in 1996." Matthew himself emphasizes from the start the personal name of Jesus by introducing it in his opening words and then mentioning it two further times in his first chapter (Mt 1:1, 16, 21). When he reaches the final chapter of his gospel he will name Jesus five times (Mt 28:5, 9, 10, 16, 18). Obviously the name of "Jesus" came easily to this early Christian writer. He would like his readers to follow suit and let "Jesus" spontaneously enter their spoken and unspoken prayers. The name enters not only Matthew's gospel but also further books of the New Testament. The entire New Testament introduces the name of Jesus 993 times. Matthew stands foursquare with other early Christians in his love for this name.

Once upon a time in some very biblically oriented schools, pupils were obliged to learn by heart Matthew's genealogy. This happened to an acquaintance of mine, now long since dead. Denis thought of these seventeen verses that he committed to memory as a piece of useless furniture stored in the attic of his mind. But the day came when he was speaking to a crowd about the claims of Jesus and the Christian faith. An irritating heckler defied him to prove that Jesus was truly the long-awaited King of the Jews. Denis fixed his eyes on the man and, to the immense delight of the crowd, recited from memory the whole of Matthew's genealogy. Its day had finally come.

Without realizing what he was doing, the heckler had moved close to two vital themes: the genuine Jewishness and full humanity of Jesus. Divine providence saw to it that the Christian Scriptures began with one of the most Jewish books in the New Testament, Matthew's gospel.

The whole gospel makes an ideal bridge between Judaism and the faith inspired by Jesus and his history. Its opening genealogy highlights the origins of Jesus, whose royal descent set him at the heart of the Jewish faith. Thank God, nowadays Christians are ready to use the title "Jesus the Jew" and have learned to appreciate that he must be understood within the whole history that stems from Abraham and Sarah. Like other male descendants of Abraham and Sarah, he was circumcised and given his name eight days after being born. When he grew up, he attended the synagogue; he prayed the psalms and other Jewish prayers; he thought and expressed himself in a Jewish way; he was steeped in the Jewish Scriptures; he honored the great sign of divine presence, the Jerusalem Temple. By reciting Jesus' genealogy, Denis was in fact joining Matthew in acknowledging Jesus' Jewishness, which for Christians must be something much more than a mere historical fact from the past. Jesus' book of prayer, the psalms, remains *the* book from which millions of Christians draw each day for their public and private prayer. The celebration of the Eucharist, the heart of Christian worship, comes from the feast of the Passover and takes its pattern at least in part from Jewish liturgy. The first and longer section of the inspired Scriptures that should guide the common and individual lives of Christians derive from pre-Christian, Jewish writers. All Christians should esteem and cherish Jewish men and women as being in a quite special way the brothers and sisters of

Jesus. They show us his face and bring us his presence. Some of the names in Matthew's genealogy are familiar enough: millions of Christians are called Ruth, David or Joseph. Some of the names such as Salathiel, Azor and Zadok are strangely unfamiliar. But all the names in Matthew's genealogy should roll joyfully off the lips of Christians. These names recall Jesus and so too do all the names of our Jewish friends today.

The man who heckled Denis, by raising the issue of Jesus' being the long-awaited king born from the house of David, also brought up the issue of Jesus' genuine humanity. After all, birth and death are two moments which clearly establish that we belong to the human race. All human beings are born and die. For some Central American death squads it has not been enough to kill their victims; they have destroyed as well the records of their birth and baptism. This is a brutal way of wiping out all memory of them and denying that they are truly human, enjoy unconditional value and share in our common history. Ever so much more than statistics are involved when we enter the names of the newly born in official registers and announce their arrival in the newspapers.

Nowadays we do less than Matthew and introduce into our records only the names of the parents: "To Cecilia and Edward Farrugia a daughter, Hildegard." Birth notices supply merely the start of a genealogical table, something that can be filled out later by those motivated to do so. Once we do so and go back a number of generations, sooner or later we will come across not only some shining exemplars like Ruth (who deserves having a biblical book named after her) but also some scoundrels and such awful tragedies as the adultery and murder that led to David's fathering Solomon. Then strange episodes turn up, such as Tamar's bold action in allowing herself to be taken to be a cult prostitute and so securing the birth of one of Jesus' ancestors, Perez (Gn 38:1–30). Like that of other human beings, Jesus' lineage has its bright side and its shadow side.

Pondering Matthew's concentrated opening chapter, we may find plenty of food for our Advent journey. Two last themes invite our attention. First, right from the start Matthew wants us to recognize that in Jesus we are expecting someone who is good news for everyone: for all women and for all men, for Jews and Gentiles alike. Right through his gospel the evangelist will make that point. But he first brings it subtly right into the opening verses. Jewish men hold together much of the genealogy, but we must not ignore Ruth, Uriah the Hittite, his wife Bathsheba and other Gentile women in Jesus' lineage. Jesus is coming to bring salvation to all human beings. Like many good writers, Matthew will pick up this opening point at the end of his gospel; there Jesus sends out his disciples to announce his good news to all peoples (Mt 28:18–20).

The final mandate given by the risen Jesus will include the instruction to "baptize in the name of the Father, and of the Son, and of the Holy Spirit." Once again we meet a theme that has already been announced right at the start of the gospel: the God to be revealed by Jesus is tripersonal. Twice Matthew states that Jesus was conceived through the power of the Holy Spirit (Mt 1:18, 20), and then he applies to Jesus a verse from Hosea to remind his readers that in Jesus we face God the Son (Mt 2:15). From the very outset the evangelist highlights the trinitarian face of Jesus' story; from beginning to end it unfolds the history of the tripersonal God's dealing with us. In Advent, as in all other seasons, we glorify the Trinity: glory be to the Father who sends us Jesus, to the Son born among us as Mary's child, and to the Holy Spirit who set going the human existence of the Son in Mary's womb. Undoubtedly the fully deployed Christian doctrine of the Trinity is not yet clearly there either in Matthew or in any other book of the New Testament. Nevertheless the evangelist helps to lay the foundation for this trinitarian faith. One might sum up his opening message as follows: this Advent let yourself think about the birth of Jesus as the coming among us and for us of God who is Father, Son and Holy Spirit.

Chapter Four:
St. Luke, Our Guide for Advent

Once you leave the eastern coast of Australia, cross the Dividing Range and head west, you will see how much of that island-continent is very flat. In what we call the "outback," you can see for many miles, off to a distant horizon or line at which the earth and sky appear to meet. Growing up "down under" made me appreciate what I was to hear in my thirties from German philosophers when I came "up over." They wrote and spoke of our mental horizon of expectation, our interior frame of mind that deals with the shape of things to come. We anticipate things and hope that our future experience will live up to or even go beyond our expectations. Some of those philosophers also revamped a theme from ancient Greek thought, the deep link between memory and expectation. Our expectations are grounded in our memories; we hope for what we remember. Prisoners in concentration camps, by recalling life before arrest, discover the strength to yearn for freedom and stay alive until it comes.

St. Luke is no philosopher, but he does encourage us to experience in Advent a time for the broadest horizons, a season when we look backwards and forwards as far as our spiritual eyes will take us. The genealogy he supplies for Jesus goes right back behind Abraham to Adam and the very creation of the human race (Lk 3:23–38). At the end of his two-volume work Luke pictures St. Paul a prisoner in Rome proclaiming Jesus and "the kingdom of God" (Acts 28:23, 31), that divine reign to be consummated at the final, public coming of Jesus. The evangelist promotes the widest possible perspectives for our Advent thoughts. Our memory takes us back to Adam, Eve and the dawn of everything; our expectations lead us forward to the crowning glory of the end. Luke offers in Advent a horizon that links heaven and earth in an enormous vista that stretches from the origin of all things right through to their glorious completion at the end.

Luke fashions the right mood for those who contemplate this cosmic vista: unbounded gratitude at the divine dealings with us and for us. He achieves this effect by bringing together in the overture to his gospel an exceptional collection of prayers: from Mary's *Magnificat* (Lk 1:46–55), through Zechariah's *Benedictus* (Lk 1:68–79) and the song of the angels (Lk 2:14), to Simeon's *Nunc Dimittis* (Lk 2:29–32). No other section of the New Testament is anything like as rich with prayer, and Luke's prayers thrill with the praise of God and deep thanksgiving at what we have received. They set the tone for what is to follow. It is as if Luke were saying to us: "Please make these prayers your own. You will truly appreciate the whole story that unfolds after my two opening chapters if you read it praising and thanking God in the spirit of Mary, Zechariah, the angels and Simeon.

The evangelist's advice might prompt us to use Advent to examine our prayer life. As we wait for the coming of Jesus, how are we praying? In particular, is there enough praise and thanksgiving when we allow our minds and hearts to be lifted to God. We could well take a cue from Mary's *Magnificat*. She moves from celebrating what God has done for her personally (Lk 1:46–50) to expressing praise for the divine power, love and fidelity shown toward all people. Why not do the same—praising God for all the blessings we and *others* have received?

Gratitude and praise give rise to and strengthen feelings of joy and gladness. Common experience repeatedly shows how a peaceful joy will pervade the lives of those who habitually say "thank you" to God and to their fellow human beings. In his first two chapters Luke keeps coming back to the theme of joy and gladness, the natural accompaniment of that spirit of gratitude he wishes to foster. The angel Gabriel announces to Zechariah the birth of a son (John the Baptist) and assures him: "His birth will fill you with joy and delight, and will bring gladness to many" (Lk 1:14). When Mary visits her cousin, Elizabeth tells her: "When your greeting sounded in my ears, the baby in my womb leapt for joy" (Lk 1:44). Mary responds in prayer: "My spirit has rejoiced in God my Savior" (Lk 1:47). The neighbors of Elizabeth share her "delight" at the birth of John (Lk 1:58). The climax of all these expressions of delight and gladness arrives when Jesus himself is born and an angel of the Lord proclaims to the shepherds this "news of great joy" (Lk 2:10). When we praise, thank and glorify God for all that has come to us through Jesus and his birth, we too will inevitably feel joy, even indescribable joy. Why not make a spiritual experiment this Advent? Try praising and thanking God much more, and then see how you feel. Luke highlights his message here not only by repeatedly coming back to the theme of praise and joy during the gospel but also by taking it up again in the very closing verse of his gospel. After the risen Jesus took them out to Bethany and then parted from them, the disciples "returned to Jerusalem full of *joy,* and spent all their time in the temple *praising* God" (Lk 24:52–53). Picking up this theme at the end is more than a mark of good writing; it shows us that Luke wishes to make a keynote idea out of praise and joy.

Years ago at a summer school in Vermont, I was struck by a particular emphasis that emerged from a lecture given for all the students by a colleague: "What we need nowadays are not hearing aids but listening aids." Recently I had the privilege of reading a manuscript by a priest who has spent a lifetime in what he calls "the ministry of listening." Clearly he has been an instrument of grace for thousands by the life-giving way he attentively listens to those who seek help. My own experience is that the best listeners are deeply grateful people. Sadly, those who consistently indulge in self-pity and never find things to their liking do not prove front-runners in paying serious attention to others. My experience supports detecting a firm link between Luke's message of praise and that of listening.

The supreme listener in Luke's opening chapter is the Blessed Virgin herself. She hears what God says to her through Gabriel in the annunciation scene and responds: "I am the Lord's servant. May it be as you have said" (Lk 1:38). A few verses later she is blessed by Elizabeth for her unique motherhood, but even more for listening and consenting to God's promise: "God's blessing is upon you above all women, and his blessing is on the fruit of your womb....Happy is she who has had faith that the Lord's word to her would be fulfilled!" (Lk 1:42, 45). Luke also portrays Mary as one who listens to other human beings. After the shepherds have related all that they had heard from the angels, "she treasures all these things and ponders over them" (Lk 2:19). She reacts in the same way twelve years later when hearing the words of her son who has remained behind in the temple on a visit to Jerusalem (Lk 2:51). Not surprisingly, it is only Luke who inserts in his gospel the comment Jesus makes when a woman in the crowd calls out, "Happy the womb that carried you and the breasts that suckled you!" Jesus' reply converges with what we have heard from Elizabeth back in chapter 1 of Luke's gospel. Mary is to be treasured for her physical motherhood, but even more for her being one who hears the word of God with persevering faith. Jesus says: "Happy are those who hear the word of God and keep it" (Lk 11:27–28). Mary, supreme listener to the divine word, help us to open ourselves to what God will say to us this Advent.

Hearing the divine message went so far in Mary's case that she conceived in her womb the Word of God in person. This is the high point in Luke's run up to the story of the birth of Jesus. To be sure, in terms of Gabriel's first pronouncement and his human ancestry, Jesus will receive "the throne of his father David, and he will be king over Israel forever" (Lk 1:32–33; see 2 Sm 7:8–16). But the second pronouncement of the angel makes clear that Mary can expect someone who is not simply a royal leader who will fulfill the promise made long ago to David. His identity takes him beyond the merely human: "The Holy Spirit will come upon you, and the power of the Most High will overshadow you; for that reason the holy child to be born will be called Son of God" (Lk 1:35).

What Luke has done here resembles what we noticed in Matthew's story of Jesus' birth and infancy. Most probably both Luke and Matthew knew Mark's gospel, in which at the baptism of Jesus God's voice declares him to be his Son and the Holy Spirit descends on him to enable him to begin his ministry with power (Mk 1:9–11). Matthew and Luke provide a flashback to the birth of Jesus and declare that he is to be acknowledged as the Son of God right from the beginning of his earthly existence. As much as or even more than Matthew, Luke appreciates the place and presence of the Trinity in the conception and birth of Jesus. Some Christian artists introduce signs and symbols of the Father and the Holy Spirit when they paint the scene of Jesus' birth in Bethlehem. Luke would agree. We do well to look forward through Advent and see in the nativity not only the Son sharing with us his holy and loving presence, but also through him the Father and the Holy Spirit doing the same.

Chapter Five:
St. John, Our Guide for Advent

St. Mark equates "the beginning of the good news of Jesus" (Mk 1:1) with his baptism and the start of his preaching. As we saw, Matthew and Luke introduce a flashback to the conception and birth of Jesus. One might add that through the genealogies which they provide, they take matters back even earlier: to Abraham and Sarah (Matthew) and to Adam and Eve (Luke). John moves things back even further by introducing a flashback to the very beginning: "In the beginning was the Word, and the Word was with God, and the Word was God. He was in the beginning with God" (Jn 1:1-2). In the course of history the Word would "become flesh" by taking on a human existence. But in and from the beginning, he was and is personally divine.

There is an unmistakable serenity to John's first eighteen verses, which announce the great truths about Jesus. In a world of curious, tormented and cynical people, these truths shine forth: from "In the beginning was the Word" through to "the Word became flesh and lived among us....It is God the only Son, who is close to the Father's heart, who has made him known."

John's message for Advent opens with the eternal

27

point of departure, the personal preexistence of Jesus. From the start of Christianity this existence "before time began" has been one classical way of expressing his divine identity. The Jesus born among us has personally existed forever. No optional extra, belief in his personal preexistence is an essential way of recognizing his divine identity. John invites us to make a thought experiment. Our minds must climb back before the universe and its time began and confess that the Son of God was already there "prior" to anything or anyone that would be created and come into being.

John's opening verses draw together creation and redemption into one great drama of divine graciousness. Through the Word of God "all things came into being" (Jn 1:3). He has also made known God and made available God's redeeming love, which delivers us from our sorrows and our sins. He offers us the new, wholly unmerited dignity of becoming God's children (Jn 1:12). These verses summon us then to ponder together the whole divine drama of creation and redemption. They will form the gospel to be read on Christmas Day itself. We would do well to make them the food for our prayer earlier in December.

In this prologue to John's gospel, the statements succeed each other like great shafts of lightning. They do not last long but they strike home with power: "What has come into being in him was life, and the life was the light of all people. The light shines in the darkness, and the darkness did not overcome it" (Jn 1:3–5). Right from the start, John's gospel pronounces Jesus to be the light of the world and the life of the world. He is light and life for the whole world. The darkness of evil wraps itself around us, but knowing Jesus, we can be delivered and live forever in the light.

We receive this eternal life by truly "seeing" the divine glory of the One who is the Father's only Son (Jn 1:14). His redeeming love is available inexhaustibly ("grace upon grace") for all who "see" him and receive him in faith. Where John says that "we have seen his glory," it is worth filling out for ourselves the identity of the "we." Mary, Joseph, the shepherds, the wise men and all who gather to worship the newborn Jesus will see and experience in him the unbounded redeeming love of God. Christmas cribs will supply for us the right image when we join the company of all those millions who have gone on seeing in the baby carried in Mary's arms One who is also God the Son and who has always been "close to the Father's heart" in a complete and eternal communion of love.

John's gospel summons us to "see" in Jesus the divine glory that comes among us. We might describe this gospel as one long act in which the glory of God is experienced and contemplated in Jesus. It begins with the community's witness to their personal experience of the incarnate Word—"We have seen his glory"—and draws to a close with Thomas gazing at the risen Jesus and confessing, "My Lord and my God" (Jn 20:28). This confession can also prompt us to look at the newborn Jesus and say, "My Lord and my God."

Like so much in this gospel, the prologue of John obviously came out of prayer and can easily be turned back into prayer. We might make of it all an Advent litany to guide our Christmas preparation.

You are the Word of God.

You were in the beginning with God. All things came into being through you.

You are the light and life of all people.

You are the true light which enlightens everyone.

You are the Word become flesh.

You are the Father's only Son, full of grace and truth.

From your fullness we have all received.

You are God the only Son, close to the Father's heart.

In this way we might turn the opening verses into a heart-to-heart conversation with the Jesus for whom we are waiting with faith and love. This Advent we can meet him in the heart of our being.

Chapter Six:
John the Baptist, Mary and Joseph

One strategy for letting ourselves be taken through Advent is to spend time with one of the principal figures from the opening chapters of the gospels. The four gospel writers begin with devout persons who faithfully further the holy Jewish traditions and now expect God to change a sinful and suffering situation.

1. Luke might lead us to spend time with John the Baptist. The age of Elizabeth and Zechariah seems to have made the birth of a child impossible. They were getting on in years. But God creates possibilities that are, humanly speaking, out of the question. As in the case of Jesus, the name of "John" is given from heaven (Lk 1:13, 60, 63); it means "God has shown favor." By announcing his birth and giving his name, Gabriel specifies the mission and destiny of John. His birth means that God has shown favor to his aging parents and even more so to the whole world. By immediately preparing the way for Jesus, John will prove to be the means of God showing favor to all people.

We are probably familiar with some painting in which John features: perhaps one in which he is a child at the side of Jesus, or perhaps one in which he is an adult engaged in baptizing Jesus. In either case, God favors us by using John to show us Jesus and lead us to Jesus.

Like the works of art we know, Advent puts before our eyes John, not only at his conception and birth, but also later, when his preaching and baptism of repentant sinners prepare the way of the Lord. John proves a double-sided figure. He chooses loneliness and belongs to the desert and its rocks. But we glimpse him also with crowds of repentant sinners by the waters of the River Jordan. A rocky wilderness and fertile waters blend strangely to shape the image of John. Matthew (3:3) follows Mark (1:6) in telling us that John's food was locusts and wild honey. Serious commentators account for this unusual diet by proposing that John avoided meat and wine and ate nothing but this poor food for ascetic reasons. Or else they attribute his diet to a desire to preserve ritual purity. In his Jesus novel, *The Gospel According to the Son* (1997) Norman Mailer playfully suggests that the "locusts could devour all the disbelief in the hearts of those who came to John. And the wild honey gave warmth to his voice when he spoke in the words of Isaiah: 'The crooked shall be made straight and the rough ways smooth'" (p. 31). Whatever we make of John's fare, this wild food was hardly a full and well-balanced diet. It raises for us a question: would a little fasting during Advent be one means of expressing repentance for our sins and preparing the way of the Lord?

2. Every Advent obviously recalls Mary's first Advent

and those last weeks of her pregnancy when she is heavy with Jesus. Yet the prescribed readings also take us back to an earlier stage in her pregnancy and a visit to Elizabeth that brings together the two mothers-to-be. As they wait for their sons to be born, they joyfully praise the greatness of God's love that they have experienced through the new life growing within them. By focusing on two pregnant women, the scene of the visitation, at least as much as the other scenes connected with Jesus' conception and birth, gives the whole story a feminine face.

The official prayers of Advent introduce a feminine title for the unborn Jesus himself: "O *Wisdom,* you come forth from the mouth of the Most High. You fill the universe and hold all things together in a strong yet gentle manner. Come and teach us the way of truth." This is the first of the "O-Antiphons" or "Greater Antiphons," which are sung before and after the *Magnificat* at Evening Prayer on the seven days preceding Christmas Eve: that is to say, from 17 to 23 December. Well over a thousand years old, these antiphons derive their name from their initial "O": "O Wisdom," "O Adonai," and so on through to "O Emmanuel" (on 23 December). The first of them evokes Wisdom as personifying, like "the Word of God" (who is echoed by saying, "you come forth from the mouth of the Most High"), the divine activity (1) in creating and sustaining in existence the whole of creation, and (2) in teaching human beings "the way of truth." The Jewish

Scriptures describe divine Wisdom as gloriously beautiful (Wis 7:22–8:1). In her teaching role Lady Wisdom
builds herself a house and invites the unwise or simple
to her rich feast (Prv 9:1–6). In a reading assigned to 17
December, Pope Leo the Great (*Epistola* 31.2–3) not
only writes of "the Word become flesh" in Mary's
womb, but also draws on Proverbs to picture the
unborn Jesus as "Wisdom building a house for herself."

Later in the story Luke will report how the boy Jesus
grows up "filled with wisdom" (Lk 2:40); in Nazareth,
Jesus' fellow countrymen will be astonished "at the
wisdom given him" (Mk 6:2). Through his parables
and sayings he will teach wisdom (e.g., Mt 25:1–12);
he will show himself to be wiser than Solomon, the
paradigm of wisdom in Old Testament history (Mt
12:42). Paul will name the crucified and risen Jesus as
"the wisdom of God" (1 Cor 1:24). In language that
recalls how the Book of Wisdom praises the radiant
beauty of Lady Wisdom, Hebrews call Jesus "the radi-
ance of God's glory" (Heb 1:3).

The first "O-Antiphon" prompts us to think of Mary
as pregnant with divine Wisdom. O Jesus, come and
teach us the way of truth; feed us with your wisdom.
Let us fall in love with your radiant beauty.

During his ministry Jesus will have much to say; in the
opening chapters of Luke, Mary has something to say.
Let us now turn to someone who has nothing to say.

3. An old saying assures us that "deeds speak louder
than words." Sometimes we may doubt that; the good

words we say can seem more important and effective than the good deeds we do. We come out with amusing stories and make others laugh. When we tell our parents, brothers, sisters and special friends how much we love them, we make them feel happy. Yet St. Joseph, a key figure in Matthew's first chapters, quietly verifies the principle that deeds speak louder than words. In those two chapters (and for that matter in Luke's opening chapters) Joseph never says a word. He says nothing when the angel tells him that Mary's baby has been conceived through the power of the Holy Spirit and that he is to call the child "Jesus." When an innkeeper tells Joseph that there is no place for him and his pregnant wife, Joseph is not credited with saying anything in reply. A little later in Luke's account, shepherds arrive to find "Mary, Joseph and the child" (Lk 2:16) and communicate their encounter with angels out in the fields. But Joseph holds his peace. He says nothing in Matthew's narrative when wise men come on the scene with a surprise packet of presents for the baby. Then an angel disturbs Joseph's sleep with the command to leave at once to Egypt. Without a word, he gets up and moves out that night with Mary and the child. After some time in Egypt (are they already becoming used to life there?), an angel disturbs Joseph's sleep once again and orders him to move back north; yet another dream leads him to take Mary and Jesus even further north, up to Nazareth in Galilee. During all of this action Joseph says nothing. We will not be surprised later (in Luke's gospel this time), when it is

Mary and not Joseph who speaks when they track down the boy Jesus after a three-day search: "Child, why have you treated us like this? Look, your father and I have been searching for you in great anxiety" (Lk 2:48).

If you want to name the strong silent man of the gospels, it has to be Joseph. We do not hear a single word from him, but we read about a fair number of things he does. He is a doer, not a speaker. He reminds us that the things we do for God and other human beings may be much more significant than the words we utter. In a different context St. Paul will write: "If I speak in the tongues of men and of angels, but do not have love, I am a noisy gong or a clanging cymbal" (1 Cor 13:1). The apostle's entire hymn to love (1 Cor 13:1–13) deserves to be applied to Joseph, the loving doer par excellence for Advent and Christmas.

Chapter Seven:
The Fifth Gospel, Our Guide for Advent

"What do you think of the Jesus Seminar and their book, *The Five Gospels?* Are they right in making much of the apocryphal gospel of Thomas?" These questions have dogged me since the early nineties. "I feel sad about so much wasted effort," I have often replied. Sometimes I have added: "After the Holocaust and after the discovery of the Dead Sea Scrolls I am amazed that they can come up with a Jesus who is less Jewish and more akin to the kind of Greek Cynic philosopher that Nietzsche portrayed him as being. I have all kinds of academic problems with their work and its results, even if I remain very grateful to their founder. Years ago he gave me helpful hints about teaching methods."

What I might also have pointed out was that the true fifth gospel has to be the Book of Isaiah. It really comes into its liturgical own during Advent and at Christmas. In many places performances of Handel's *Messiah* let wonderful texts from Isaiah ring in our ears and resonate in our hearts. We first hear "Comfort ye, my people," for "every valley shall be exalted" and "the glory of the Lord shall be revealed." Then the alto and the chorus sing: "O thou that tellest good tidings to Zion." We are ready to listen to the chorus: "For unto us a child is born, unto us a Son is given."

Hence I want to suggest that our Advent prayer and reflection may be properly fueled by the Book of Isaiah, as well as by Mark 1, Matthew 1-2, Luke 1-3 and John 1. Let me pick out four themes from Isaiah that seem peculiarly helpful in December.

First, we all rejoice in those poetic texts about the ideal king who is to come: "Unto us a child is born, unto us a Son is given." We who walk in darkness have seen a great light. We will be led by a wise Ruler who is divine in might, who will constantly show fatherly care and love, and who will bring peace and prosperity: "He is named Wonderful Counselor, Mighty God, Everlasting Father, Prince of Peace" (Is 9:2-7). Wisdom and justice will characterize this anointed King; the Spirit of the Lord will rest upon him. Nature itself will share in the coming harmony and idyllic peace: "The wolf shall live with the lamb, the leopard shall lie down with the kid, the calf and the lion and the fatling together, and a little child shall lead them" (Is 11:1-9). These promises enjoy a lovely fulfillment in the kingdom that Jesus has inaugurated and will see through to completion. We know that in him the promise has been realized for us: "Your eyes will see the king in his beauty" (Is 33:17).

Second, when the people are brought home from exile, Isaiah knows that they will be consoled by their tender and compassionate God. The divine glory will be revealed when God comes with might and gentleness:

"He will feed his flock like a shepherd; he will gather the lambs in his arms, and carry them in his bosom, and gently lead the mother sheep" (Is 40:1–11). Deliverance comes with power from "the Lord your God, the Holy One of Israel, your Savior" (Is 43:3). Yet this same God protects and watches over the exiled people with unique fondness: "Do not fear, for I have redeemed you; I have called you by name, you are mine. When you pass through the waters, I will be with you; and through the rivers, they shall not overwhelm you" (Is 43:1–2). Motherly love naturally serves to express the delicate, utterly faithful love of God our Comforter and Redeemer: "Can a woman forget her nursing child, or show no compassion for the child of her womb? Even these may forget, yet I will not forget you. See, I have inscribed you on the palms of my hands" (Is 15–16). Nowhere can we find gentler and more tender images of God our Creator and Redeemer.

The gathering of the Israelites and of all people is a further theme to ponder, especially in the second half of Isaiah. In a new and greater exodus, the people of God will be brought home and restored (for example, Is 43:14–44:5). More than that, all nations are invited to bow down before God and sing the divine praises (45:14–25). The whole world must come and join in the song of praise: "Sing to the Lord a new song, his praise from the end of the earth" (Is 42:10). When around the world old and young from all races gather at a Christmas crib and sing their carols, the homecoming theme of Isaiah finds a special, poignant fulfillment. In the stories of Matthew and Luke, the wise men, the angels and the shepherds anticipate us in this cosmic home-coming, that gathering around Jesus to sing the divine praises, which will bring all human beings home to God.

Fourth, an unmistakable moral seriousness marks the Book of Isaiah. It begins with a series of oracles aimed at correcting the sinful superficiality of the people (Is 1:2–31). God passes judgment on the arrogant, the corrupt and those who falsely challenge moral standards by attempting to justify evil actions. The sinful and selfish are called to care for orphans, widows, the poor and other powerless individuals. Isaiah's prophetic call highlights the utterly holy God, who is ready to cleanse and forgive human failure (Is 6:1–13).

The Jesus Seminar has prized and overvalued a second-century, somewhat decadent work, the so-called *Gospel of Thomas,* making of it a fifth gospel alongside Matthew, Mark, Luke and John. Advent, more than all the other seasons of the year, suggests, rather, discovering in Isaiah "the fifth gospel." Treasured by Jews and Christians alike, this prophetic book has proved itself good news over and over again. Its majestic and sensitive image of God, along with a many-dimensioned spiritual message, means that it can wonderfully nourish our spirits in the days that lead to Christmas and the New Year.

CHRISTMAS

Chapter Eight:
Interpreting Christmas

The birth of Jesus is a profound reality that defies some simple interpretation confined to just one context. It does not present quite the same face in the settings of study, life and prayer. Scholars, sufferers and worshipers rightly appropriate the Christmas story in a variety of ways.

Immanuel Kant's *Critique of Pure Reason* may seem of little interest to any but the philosophers. Yet that classic work ends with three questions which retain a permanent validity everywhere. "What can I know? What ought I to do? What may I hope for?"

Those questions readily suggest three major lines of inquiry about the Christmas story. What can I know about the historical formation and theological meaning of the infancy narratives in the first two chapters of the gospels according to Matthew and Luke? What ought I to do or leave undone when the story of Jesus' birth reads off the movement of my life? What may I hope for when that story becomes my prayer?

The first question invites us to station ourselves in a place of biblical and theological thought—let us say, the University of Notre Dame, Yale Divinity School or the Gregorian University. The second question takes us off to the world of action and suffering, like the suburbs of Sâo Paulo. The final question could turn us toward the Church of the Nativity in Bethlehem.

Let us first join the scholars and students in their academic setting. Here we join a community whose tradition—at least in the Western world—stretches back through the enlightenment and the achievements of medieval Europe to the glories of ancient Greece. Plato's conversational approach has shaped this tradition for all time. We raise questions, concede points and draw conclusions as the dialogue runs along. Error is the villain, and carefully trained reason the solution in this rigorous pursuit of truth.

The intellectual approach to Christmas scrutinizes the intentions of Matthew and Luke, searches out the sources they used and tries to tell at this distance the precise historical events that first gave rise to their stories about Jesus' conception, birth and babyhood. In the best sense of the word "theory," biblical scholars have their theories about the meaning, formation and origins of the infancy narratives. They focus on the past in seeking to verify their answers to such questions as: Where did the story of the wise men come from and what did Matthew mean by it? Did the Romans take that census (Lk 2:1–5) and was Jesus really born in Bethlehem? What are Luke's major concerns in his opening chapters?

Theories are judged by one's competent use of the available evidence. Truth has the primacy when exegetes practice their academic discipline. Theirs is the work of an intellectual elite. They have enjoyed a privileged education as the heirs to the great tradition formed by the old universities of Bologna, Cambridge, Heidelberg, Oxford and Paris.

A second view of Jesus' birth comes from the *favelas,* where people suffer terrible deprivation and struggle to survive. Here it is a matter of consulting the poor, not the scholars, about the meaning and message of Christmas. In this setting it is not so much intellectual error but injustice, poverty and sin that stand in the way of appropriating the story of Jesus' birth.

Stripped to its simplest terms, Christmas here means something to be lived and done. The mystery of the Word of God dwelling among us as a newborn child calls for a transformation of our world. It invites those who suffer and those who cause their suffering to seek and find a new kind of human existence.

This second way of understanding the Christmas story challenges us to "repent and believe in the good news of Jesus' birth" rather than "interpret the infancy narratives more scientifically." We justify and verify the story of Bethlehem more by practicing it than by studying it.

The second approach is focused on the here and now—on the present history of suffering, sin and evil. Its vision of Christmas takes shape around the questions: What good ought I to do for all those for whom Jesus was born into the world?

The wise men from the East symbolize a third approach to the "silent and holy night" of Christmas. They follow their star to come and worship the newborn Savior of the world (Mt 2:1-2). They represent all those whose hearts continue to catch fire at the child in the manger, that exquisitely beautiful expression of the divine love for us all. On our knees with the Magi we glimpse the grandeur of God who comes among us to "save his people from their sins" (Mt 1:21).

Contemplating the newborn child, we know that "the hopes and fears of all the years" find their answer in him. We need fear no more, but can hope that we are on our way home to a God who cherishes us with everlasting love.

Such then are three different but complementary approaches to the Christmas story: through our head, our hands and our heart. The scholar studies and analyzes the story for its historical and theological truth. Those who suffer and struggle in the marketplace can let the story enter and enrich their lives like Luke's poor shepherds who "watched their flocks by night" (Lk 2:8). Finally, the faithful take in the story when they come rejoicing to worship our newborn king. He appeared among us as Mary's tiny baby, but will come again as Lord to take us to himself.

Christmas is the story of the child who holds out to us the full and final answers in our triple quest for what we can know, what we ought to do, and what we may hope for. We can encounter that child in the university setting, along the roads of life and in our places of prayer. In him we find the plenitude of truth, the ultimate good and the utterly satisfying beauty of God. It will take all our study, life and worship to know him.

Chapter Nine:
Knowing the Christmas Story

What is it to "know" the Christmas story? Who really knows it best? To vary matters, let us hear not only from scholars but also from children and saints.

Scholars have their advantages. They fill their libraries with dictionaries, grammars, critical editions of the New Testament and biblical commentaries in any number of foreign languages. They can study and speculate about the sources that Matthew and Luke might have used in their accounts of the conception and birth of Jesus. They come up with helpful insights about the intentions and perspectives of the gospel writers themselves; they can tell us a great deal about the social, political and religious situations in the Holy Land at the time Jesus was born, as well as about the situation in the Mediterranean world when Matthew and Luke wrote. Scholars know a great deal *about* the gospel texts. Many of them also know personally and deeply the child presented by Matthew and Luke for our love and adoration. But not all of them.

Some scholars even make a virtue of taking their distance from faith when scrutinizing the Christmas texts. They do their work in the name of impartial, disengaged reason. They do not want to share personally in the story or insert their own being in the act of interpreting the opening chapters of Matthew and Luke. They can produce some detailed results about the context, sources and composition of the Christmas stories, but hardly any spiritual insights into the mission and message of the baby whose coming is celebrated by those stories. This "neutral" approach can seem just a little like analyzing the plays of Shakespeare while sedulously ignoring their poetry and drama. Some scholars may need to hear the words of Martin Luther: "Think of the Scriptures as...the richest of mines which can never be sufficiently explored, in order that you may find that divine wisdom which God here lays before you in such simple guise as to quench all pride. Here you will find the swaddling cloths and the manger in which Christ lies....Simple and lowly are these swaddling cloths, but dear is the treasure, Christ, who lies in them."

Luther insisted as much as anyone in Christian history that Jesus himself is at the center of the Scriptures and is the focus of the whole narrative which we know best with our hearts: the story of Christmas. This is a story that children know with their hearts when they turn into Mary, Joseph, angels, shepherds, the innkeeper or the Magi, and put on a nativity play. When they go on the stage at Christmas, sing in their school choirs or dress up for midnight mass, the energy and holy simplicity of children can spark some spontaneous insights that astonish adults by their sensitivity.

A catechist facing a gathering of local families once asked: "If you were going away on a long journey, what would you want to leave behind so that people could remember you best?" The grownups and teenagers present gave the answers one might expect: "You would leave behind a good photograph of yourself, a letter you had written, or a scarf you had worn." But then a seven-year-old girl took their breath away by saying, "You would leave yourself." That is just what Jesus did at the first Christmas. He did not send us a photograph or something he had written. He came in person and then left us himself.

In 1995 many people remembered and celebrated the fourth centenary of the martyrdom of St. Robert Southwell (1561–95). While imprisoned for nearly three years, he was constantly racked and tortured, before being hung, drawn and quartered at Tyburn. Southwell's life and ministry were short, as was the case with Christ himself. But the martyr's voice lives on in the poems that have gone into edition after edition. He praised and glorified God for the birth of Jesus in poems of particular passion and energy like "The Burning Babe," "New Heaven, New War," and "The Nativity of Christ" with its closing stanza:

Man altered was by sin from man to beast;

Beast's food is hay, hay is all mortal flesh.

Now God is flesh and lies in manger pressed

As hay, the brutest sinner to refresh.

O happy field wherein this fodder grew,

Whose taste doth us from beasts to men renew.

Nearly four hundred years before Robert Southwell, another saint, Francis of Assisi, left the world in his debt by celebrating Christmas very concretely: in a barn with animals and straw. He wanted to illustrate and share the nativity story in the way that he knew it best—in his own life. He stamped on the world's imagination the place of Christ's birth: an outhouse for animals that is radiant with divine light.

Thanks to St. Francis and his followers, Italy is still awash with all kinds of cribs at Christmas time. If you study the faces of all those who turn up in Rome and pray before the image of the newborn child, you will find scholars, children and saints side by side on their knees. Together they remember and know the One who left himself behind. We need scholars, children and saints to tell us what Christmas is like and what Christmas is about. After all, Christmas is a matter for our heads, for our hearts and for our lives.

Chapter Ten:
On First Seeing Bethlehem

It was after sunset when I first reached Tantur, the Ecumenical Institute for Theological Research which sits on a rise south of Jerusalem. Down the road the lights of Bethlehem shone at me through the warm August darkness. High above the town the evening star glittered in the sky.

Next morning the muezzin from a nearby mosque woke me just after 4 A.M. I slept again but fitfully till the bells from the Christian churches announced the dawn. Then the sun came up over the hills of Moab to show me Bethlehem. I lifted my eyes across the olives and cypresses to the towers and spires of David's "royal city." In the left distance a flat-topped cone drew my attention. It was Herodion, the hill where Herod the Great built a citadel and where later they brought his body for burial. To the right a new Israeli settlement, Gilo, crowned another hill like a latter-day crusader castle.

After breakfast I sat on my tiny balcony to face Bethlehem and say the divine office. To my delight I discovered that the Office of Readings began: "But you Bethlehem Ephrathah, the least of the clans of Judah, out of you will be born for me the One who is to rule over Israel. He will stand and feed his flock with the power of the Lord." The sight of the city itself charged Micah's prophecy with fresh meaning.

The sun had swung across the sky to the west before our meetings ended and I was free to go down to Bethlehem. Along the road I passed two shepherds. Several goats were mixed up with the flock of sheep. Until I looked closely at their heads and tails, I could not tell the goats from the sheep. I pressed on past Rachel's Tomb, where some young Israeli couples still come to seek her blessing on their marriages.

The road forked. I turned left down Manger Street and slipped aside to visit King David's Wells. Tradition associates several ancient cisterns with an incident from one of David's battles with the Philistines. Thirst made him exclaim: "O that someone would give me water to drink from the well of Bethlehem which is by the gate" (2 Sm 23:15). Three of his followers heard their king's plea and broke through the Philistine ranks to fetch him some water. But David refused to drink it because of the risk his men had taken.

Right in front of King David's Wells is a cinema where a film, *Jesus,* had been running for months. Based on Luke's gospel, it was being offered free of charge. "By this time," one of the locals told me, "it must have been seen by most of the inhabitants." "Showing a film on Jesus in Bethlehem," I commented, "seems a bit like carrying coals to Newcastle."

I hurried to Manger Square and on into the Basilica

of the Nativity. Distant organ music followed me down into the cave. A young man and woman squatted in prayer. Their silent devotion filled the place. The thought shook me and brought tears to my eyes: The Son of God really took flesh among us.

Other pilgrims drifted in. Some closed their eyes and prayed. Some read the story of Jesus' birth and sang a Christmas carol. Others simply stood there and wept.

I climbed out of the cave, slipped through the church, crossed the square and walked back along Star Street. A pregnant woman passed me. A little later another young mother came along leading a tiny, open-faced boy. I laughed for the joy of these reminders. Then I remembered how Bethlehem means "house of bread." I stopped to buy a fragrant roll. It sustained me on the climb back up the road to Tantur.

From the roof of the institute my gaze drifted across the stony landscape. Fifteen miles or so to the southeast, three packs of leopards still roam the Judean wilderness. They live off the ibex and other animals. Away to the north, storks, eagles and other birds of prey gather in the thousands when the shorter days drive them south from central and eastern Europe. They soar to great heights on the warm air currents and glide past Tantur on the way down to Africa. They will all have gone south by the time Christmas comes around again.

Up on the terrace of Tantur some fearful questions played on my mind: What can we expect from a world that is so good at doing evil? Will we continue to hunt each other in our tribal and national packs? Or will we simply glide away from situations that have become difficult and seemingly unbearable? The light drained out of the sky. The evening star came into view again over Bethlehem. It dreamt up the vision of a peasant woman and her tiny Son. His presence can always bring us peace. That peace does not mean the survival of the fittest but bread in the hands of the hungry.

Chapter Eleven:
Christmas at the Railway Station

As we head toward the third millennium and the great jubilee year of 2000, more and more visitors and pilgrims (including visitors who become pilgrims) are turning up in Rome. No doubt the pace of visits and pilgrimages will quicken even more so this Christmas as we move toward Christmas 1999.

During the year and not least in December, many visitors and pilgrims reach the Eternal City through the main railway station. Italian long-distance trains tend to be much more punctual now; occasionally they even arrive ahead of time. On the short run from Rome's Leonardo da Vinci Airport, hourly trains deposit passengers coming off international and intercontinental flights.

In front of the station, lines of taxis move past smoothly. Beyond, rows of buses fill the square before they depart and fan out across town. To the right you will see a section of the walls of Republican Rome, which protected the city from the early fourth century before Christ.

If you arrive at the station over Christmas time, please don't miss something special—right inside the main concourse. At first glance the huge crib suggests a scene from Naples. In fact it is a street scene from Trastevere, the old Roman quarter that lies across the Tiber from the city's center and runs along the river banks at the foot of the Janiculum hill. From early times Trastevere enjoyed an international population, the cosmopolitan flavor of a busy port. In the second or even the third century before Christ, a Jewish community settled there and eventually built a synagogue, sections of which still remain today.

Summoning up Trastevere from around 1500 A.D., the street scene in the railway crib shows exotic Magi coming upon people engaged in their daily lives. Women look down from upper-story windows; shepherds have gathered their flocks around fires; some folk are doing their washing at a fountain; traders sell their goods; little children are hard at play. At the heart of the whole scene is the newborn Jesus in his manger.

The crib's street scene may date from five hundred years ago. Yet it matches brilliantly what you will see all around it in the railway concourse. Vigorous backpackers rush by; old couples walk wearily to their trains; young Italians doing military service gather with groups of friends. Crippled people move by in wheelchairs. Nuns arrive and leave. Men and women wearing official badges offer tourists information about the city or direct them to hotels. Foxy-faced men tout gypsy cabs and other unauthorized services. Most elegantly dressed police officers stride up and down to discourage crime and encourage good order. Children pass by with their parents. A few of them are begging or looking for someone to rob. Aware of younger and older thieves, the authorities have posted a notice at strategic points around the crib: "When you are admiring the crib, please watch your possessions. Others can take advantage of your being distracted."

The warning is called for. Plenty of incoming or departing passengers stop to admire the crib's craftsmanship and smile at the Baby who is the center of it all. The sacred music playing over the station's bustle draws them there and can leave them off guard.

Yet the warning about "you" and "others" also evokes a lasting truth. Christ was born for all of us: for those who live honestly and for those who survive by stealing; for the energetic backpackers and for the elderly pensioners; for young servicemen and for the crippled; for the licensed officials and for foxy-faced touters. Jesus came for every class and condition of human beings. He wanted to be with the Jews and the Romans of two thousand years ago, and with all those represented in that Trastevere street scene from five centuries ago. He wants to share life, his life, with every person and every kind of person who passes through Rome's main railway station today.

As a Jesuit I have repeatedly made the Spiritual Exercises, in which St. Ignatius Loyola proposes the key contemplation on the incarnation, or the coming in human flesh of the Son of God. In it Ignatius invites those making the Exercises to "see all the different people on the face of the earth, so varied in dress and behavior. Some are white and others black; some at peace and others at war; some weeping and others laughing; some well and others sick; some being born and others dying." The Second Person of the Trinity took on human flesh and life to save them all. I know no better setting for that contemplation on the incarnation than a large contemporary station or, for that matter, an airport. Few places express more directly the hustle and needs of modern times than a large and lively railway station.

The crib in Rome's main station has been fashioned and maintained by Italian railway workers; it has been sponsored by a bank. We need bankers and railway workers. But, along with all of us, they too need Jesus. If you pass through that station this Christmas or next Christmas, pause for a moment and praise Jesus who has been born among us to live at the heart of our lives.

Chapter Twelve:
Surprised by Christmas

While attending Christmas mass in 1986, the American novelist Walker Percy was overtaken by a completely unexpected religious experience. He wrote about it at once to his psychiatrist friend at Harvard University, Robert Coles: "The mass was going on, the homily standard....A not-so-good choir of young rock musicians got going on 'Joy to the World', the vocals not so good but enthusiastic. Then it hit me: what if it should be the case that the entire cosmos had a Creator and what if he decided for reasons of his own to show up as a little baby, conceived and born under suspicious circumstances? Well, Bob, you can lay it to Alzheimer's or hangover or whatever, but—it hit me—I had to pretend I had an allergy attack so I could take out my handkerchief."

In his biography of Walker Percy, *Pilgrim in the Ruins*, Jay Tolson tells the story of a lifetime struggle: Percy's struggle with a wonderfully cultured but deeply shadowed Southern upbringing (his father and grandfather both committed suicide), recurrent tuberculosis, friends who could not understand his conversion to Catholicism, a persistent sense of despair within himself and frequent depression over the course his country was taking after the Second World War. That Christmas experience startled the novelist, who—as Tolson comments—"had never had anything close to a mystical experience, never even a twinge of pentecostal enthusiasm." All his life, Percy had been such an intellectual and self-controlled man, that "this completely unexpected experience of something beyond his rational ken was both gratifying and frightening."

The experience came late in Percy's life, giving him a sense of marveling amazement at the divine Word becoming flesh and dwelling among us.

The celebration of the Eucharist was a highly appropriate setting for Walker Percy to be deeply shaken by the human birth of the Son of God. In his classic poem, "Christmas," Sir John Betjeman catches the deep connection between the divine presence in the arms of Mary and in the Eucharist. Face-to-face with the newborn Jesus and with the eucharistic elements, we meet the same question: is it true that the "Maker of the stars and sea" was present then in Bethlehem and is present here and now on the altar at midnight mass? Nothing can compare with this truth—"That God was Man in Palestine / And lives today in Bread and Wine."

The humanity of God makes his Son astonishingly vulnerable. Who is more defenseless than the tiny child of a poor mother who has conceived him "under suspicious circumstances"? What presence could be more precarious and exposed than his presence in the Eucharist?

With Jesus, God drew near to us in person. God reached out, crossed the enormous gap and came as *the* gift of Christmas. Here there was and is no loving "from a distance," but rather, a love which brought the Son of God to be with us and to be one of us.

Søren Kierkegaard classically exemplified the paradoxical truth of things in his *Concluding Unscientific Postscript.* "The absurd is," he wrote, "that the eternal Truth has come into being in time, that God...has been born, has grown up and so forth, precisely like any other individual human being."

Walker Percy's long friendship with Robert Coles began with the latter probing the novelist's identity. At the end of his life Percy came to experience profoundly the way his identity was bestowed on him through the love expressed forever by the baby in Mary's arms. As a Catholic theologian I have to expound the faith, but as a Catholic Christian I would rather find myself stunned with amazement like Percy and joining him at Christmas by faking an allergy and pulling out my handkerchief.

Chapter Thirteen:
A Public Display of Affection

Some relatives of mine have long since shifted from Shepherd's Bush (London). But it was on a visit there that I first learned what "PDAs" mean. One day Sarah, the eldest of the three daughters, jokingly summed up a major feature of her family's life by saying, "There may be too many PDAs in this house." "Public displays of affection," she explained when I checked on the term.

It certainly was and is a family given to generous and frequent PDAs. They have never needed to encourage one another by leaving around the house any of those Californian "free hug coupons." Their hearts were and remain united by hugs and much else besides. Two of the girls are married now and share their hugs with wider circles of new relatives and friends.

At times the whole family has made me wonder whether God called them to exercise a ministry of hugging for the benefit of us all. At other times they have suggested my summing up the message of Christmas as a truly spectacular public display of affection on the part of God.

For all its seeming isolation, what happened in Bethlehem two thousand years ago was radically connected with all history and with the rest of the world. Mary held the newborn Jesus to her breast. But through that baby, God was embracing the world and drawing the divine arms tightly around all of us.

One summer I taught the same course on Jesus Christ three times: first in San Francisco, then on the outskirts of Dublin, and finally near Liverpool. When we came to the question of his being truly human and truly divine, the audiences on both sides of the Atlantic gave much the same answers to my question, "Why is it vital for you that Christ is human *and* divine?"

"If he were not truly human," the participants insisted, "he would not be one of us and could not represent us before God." "If he were not truly divine," they added, "he could not really do anything for us, and we would not be easily convinced that God genuinely cares for us. Only the living presence among us of God's Son proves the divine love beyond all shadow of doubt."

Those students in San Francisco, Dublin and Liverpool appreciated the point and purpose of that public display of infinite affection that was Jesus' coming to us as a human baby. It takes the perfect simplicity and unique generosity of this divine gift to make us believe that God truly loves us. God has transformed everything by passing the divine gesture of love through the tiny body held in Mary's arms.

Some time back I told a friend about my Christmas theme of PDAs. He questioned my use of "affection," pressed the claims of "love," and told me how higher-ups had tampered with the draft-report from a home for mentally handicapped people. Where the original text had spoken of "relationships motivated by love," the official report came back with "love" crossed out and replaced by "unconditional positive regard." I hope it is more than loyalty that has made me hang onto "public displays of affection"—loyalty to Sarah and, after more than twenty years in Rome, loyalty to my adopted language. In Italian, *affetto* and its derivatives can enjoy a rich and strong meaning.

Yet here, as always, context proves decisive for meaning. In the context of Sarah's family, to talk of PDAs carried and still carries obvious overtones of deep love. The same (and ever so much more) is true when we apply this term to that divine microcosm of all the world and all history, the birth of Jesus in Bethlehem.

Without the Son of God's incarnate display of affection at Mary's breast, we would be merely voices whispering in the dark and, one could well add, merely bodies hugging in the dark. Our love for one another has a completely satisfying and lasting future because of God's supreme PDA, which is the Christmas story.

Chapter Fourteen:
Filling Our Senses

Christmas evokes scores of memories—of things seen, smelt, tasted, heard and felt, year by passing year. The mind's eye can summon up some wonderful cribs, the eager faces of choirboys, the magic stocking crammed with toys, candles flickering on family tables or Santa Claus glimpsed for the first time. Our days are numbered, and we are not indispensable. But the warm glow of memory overcomes the passage of time, brings back our past Christmases and lets us see it all again.

Christmas trees have their special smell, like the resinous pines I used to cut in the back field of my parents' farm and drag to the house. Years later I caught another refreshingly distinctive scent at Christmas—that of a stately fir tree gracing a village church in northern Germany. Friends have told me how they can still sniff the cones burning in fireplaces at home, while others have spoken of the sharp scent of charred eucalyptus leaves carried on a wind across Australia from distant brushfires. These friends can smell again the fires of Christmas, cheering fires in the northern hemisphere or the threatening fires in the southern.

Christmas offers its particular tastes, like mince pies, brandy butter and mulled wine. Memory relives the savor of Christmas pudding from my childhood in Australia, when I slowly chewed a rich spoonful in search of silver pieces. The feast of Jesus' birthday enjoys its own special tastes that don't exist at other times in the year.

At Christmas we hear our favorite carols ding-donging merrily on high. A parish choir from long ago rings out again in our ear, or perhaps an innocent child's voice leads us in "Silent Night." The beloved songs we sing and hear on Christmas night have been repeated from generation to generation. They come to us enriched and sanctified by our ancestors. These carols go on binding us together in the public worship of the church and in simple domestic traditions we pass on and practice.

The bright sharpness of memory also resurrects things touched on Christmases years ago: the warm bodies of our parents as they hugged us, the feel of a new toy, the fur fringes of Santa Claus's outfit or the rough planks that made up a crib housing the Holy Family.

When we celebrate Christmas, we know that its magnificent religious symbols have not lost their meaning. Secular concerns converge with the sacred mysteries as we share memories and renew public and private rituals. By being built out of what we see, smell, taste, hear and feel, all these symbols and rituals correspond convincingly to what Christmas faith essentially means. The Word of God took on our human, fleshly nature and was born into our world. With that nativity, through our physical senses we began to take in the Son of God among us. We could, quite literally, see, hear, smell, taste and touch him.

In our mind's eye we gaze at the child as he sleeps cradled in Mary's arms. We see him, the focus of attention for Joseph and all who visit the stable. We hear the sharp cries of Jesus. We smell the fresh fragrance of the tiny baby when washed at birth. Christian art encourages us to capture the scent of the frankincense brought by the Magi and the odor of the camels they rode. We taste the sweetness of the whole story and savor the goodness of the Lord's new presence among us. Our imagination lets us feel the warmth of the baby in our own arms on the chilly night when he first came to us.

Year by year we renew our Christmas rituals and share memories of the things seen, heard, smelt, tasted and touched. The season inspires us to retell what we once experienced through our senses. Those same senses come into play at the sheer wonder of God's Son incarnated into our world and being born for all of us.

Luke's gospel says that Mary kept all her experiences of the very first Christmas alive in the memory of her heart. As the years rolled on, she could still see, hear, smell, taste and touch her newborn child. Those same senses let us, in our turn, keep track both of Christmases long ago and of our faith in God's Son come to be one of us forever. We remember what all those Christmases gave us through our senses, and confess our faith in Jesus born into the world so that we can see, hear, taste, smell and touch the unthreatening Source of our redemption.

Christmas and the incarnation bring to mind passionate love and the many memories it leaves behind— of the one seen, heard, touched, tasted and smelt. Bernard of Clairvaux, Hildegard of Bingen, Abelard, Héloïse and other medieval Christians movingly captured the human experience of love, along with a luminous, physical sense of the incarnation. No wonder we owe the Christmas crib to one of the greatest saints, Francis of Assisi. He knew how the newborn Jesus fills our senses. May Jesus fill them once again this Christmas, through our lively faith in his incarnation.

Chapter Fifteen:
Truth at Christmas

When I was on a working trip to South America in the mid-1980s, a statue from the colonial past and a speech at a congress for new businessmen suggested to me the double claim of Christmas. This feast invites us to face the full truth about God's Son and the real state of humanity.

In São Paulo a young woman guided me through a spectacular museum of religious art. We passed golden altars and chalices, many statues of Our Lady, a tiared St. Peter on a throne, and a quizzical St. George in search of some fresh dragon. We paused in front of a winged figure embracing Francis of Assisi. If you hurried by, you might have thought the heavenly being was the crucified and risen Christ appearing in seraphic form on Mount Alvernia to impress the stigmata on the body of St. Francis. Instead it was a representation of the earthly Jesus.

"If you look closely," Anita told me, "you will see that Jesus has three and not four wings. There is a hole in one shoulder where he normally folded his wings away and hid them from the public gaze." "Why did the artist picture Christ that way?" I asked. "It was because he knew some people didn't believe that the earthly Jesus was really human," she explained. "They thought of him as only an angel in disguise."

"Poor Saint Francis," I muttered. It is impossible to think of anyone who has done more to encourage believers to take seriously the real and full humanity of God's Son disclosed above all in the nativity and the crucifixion. Francis gave people everywhere the Christmas crib. In the last two years of his life his own body bore the marks of the passion and made him a vivid sign of Our Lord's true suffering. And yet here was Francis portrayed as the privileged person to whom Christ "revealed" his "real" nature as an angel in disguise!

The question raised by that unknown artist several hundred years ago is still worth putting to ourselves. Do we genuinely believe that Jesus Christ is not only truly and fully divine but also truly and fully human? If we suspect a touch of "angelism" in our attitude, praying before a crib this Christmas may prove the potent remedy.

From Brazil I went on to Chile where the first "Congress of New Businessmen" was taking place. Some fine and good things were said about the call to "place at the service" of humanity "the goods created by God." What caught my attention, however, were the remarks made by the president of the Confederation of Production and Commerce when closing the congress. "When a young man," he said, "with all the impulse of youth decides to be master of his own destiny and becomes a businessman, he begins a fascinating and hard life which constitutes a constant challenge that will accompany him right to death."

Shortly after coming across those words, I read what the Catholic bishops of Chile wrote in their "Pastoral Orientations 1986/89" about so many young Chileans who felt themselves utterly hemmed in: "They no longer have anywhere to look. For them there are no opportunities. In Chile unemployment is high, and the greatest number of unemployed is found among the young. Many cannot finish their studies. Some...leave Chile in search of better living possibilities." For very many young people "the doors of the future are closed."

The bishops also noted the results of this discouraging situation for numerous young Chileans: alcoholism, other forms of drug addiction, passive resignation, immature love relationships and violence.

When you walked the streets or rode the buses of Santiago in those days, you would see young people trying to sell shoelaces, sweets, tablemats and other bits and pieces in a desperate attempt to survive. In the suburb of La Victoria three out of five of those between the ages of fifteen and twenty-four were totally unemployed.

By the late 1990s the economic and political situation of Chile has taken an enormous turn for the better. Back in the 1980s the Chilean bishops identified the truth of the human situation in their country: a growing misery and violence that had been in large measure produced by the current government and made the youth of Chile "the most vulnerable social group" of all. It was to this bishops' statement rather than to bland claims about young men with "all the impulse of youth" deciding to be "masters of their destiny" that one looked for the truth about the real conditions then facing young Chileans.

When he embraced a leper, St. Francis pointed to the second great claim of Christmas. We should face the truth about those around us and show them the love they need.

In the end I was glad to have seen the winged Christ in Brazil and come across that address for the Congress of New Businessmen in Chile. What I saw and read recalled the two great claims of Christmas. We must acknowledge the full humanity of God's Son and recognize the real needs of the people who surround us.

Chapter Sixteen:
A Season for All Ages

Some years ago I was back in Naples, a city that
never fails to revive and astonish me with its warm
humanity. Little Chiara, fresh from her first communion, was there to welcome me. Bright and ready to go
at the age of nine, she filled me in about her lessons in
geography and English.

Young Giuseppe took time off from his work in the
Bourbon palace and guided me through the Teatro San
Carlo, the city's legendary opera house. I went up
front and tested the perfect acoustics with my render-
ing of "La donna è mobile." Then we crossed the road
to drink some excellent coffee in the huge arcade of
King Umberto I. The first evening two friends, capti-
vatingly in love with each other, took me out to a village on the Bay of Naples. After hours of delicious fish,
sparkling wine and wonderful talk, Gino and Fausta
walked me along the waterfront to lift our eyes above
the boats and see the stars.

The following day I lunched with two old men. To
entertain me they recalled with laughter and affection
highlights from their past: one his years as a tailor in
Rome, and the other a long stay in Australia that initiated

him into the dangers of surf beaches in Queensland. Yet the best of the golden oldies that day was an ancient Poor Clare sister. Angelina flashed me the greatest of smiles when we met at the entrance to the Gesù Nuovo, the most ornate of the baroque churches in Naples.

Kindness and love abound in the crowded streets of Naples. On the train back to Rome I thought about Chiara, Giuseppe, Gino, Fausta, the two old men and Angelina. For two days they had let me into their lives. On those warm days and calm evenings I had once again enjoyed the magic humanity of Neapolitans of all ages.

It made me remember something very different and very ugly that I had watched earlier that year—a television program about a country where the "then" government systematically denied medical services to the aging and elderly. They were no longer economically useful. They had to face their declining years without the care and comfort of doctors and hospitals. What happened to Jesus as he moved toward birth happened to them as they moved toward death. There was no room for them in the inn.

From a human point of view, the policy of that government was plainly and totally wrong. It would have been and would be unthinkable in Naples. From a Christian point of view, it simply did not square with the vision of the elderly that we find in Luke's infancy narratives.

The complete Christmas story, found in the first two

chapters of Luke's gospel, ranges across the human generations. The actors who are named run from a pair of newborn boys (John and Jesus himself), through a young couple (Mary and Joseph) and an older pair (Elizabeth and Zechariah) and ends with two remarkable people in their twilight years (Simeon and Anna).

We can easily slip into the habit of thinking of Christmas as a feast for children and the young. It is, after all, a season when we celebrate our newborn king. But the full cast in Luke's nativity play includes the aging, the elderly and the really old.

The gospel opens with an elderly man (Zechariah) praying and carrying out his priestly service in Jerusalem (Lk 1:5–23). Toward the end of Luke's infancy narrative we meet a very old man (Simeon) and a widow, then eighty-four years of age (Anna). Simeon is God's faithful servant personified. Now that he has seen God's salvation come among us through the presence of Jesus, he is ready to be released from duty and go home to God. Three times we are told of the role of the Holy Spirit in Simeon's life (Lk 2:25–27). It is through the Holy Spirit that he finds Mary and Joseph, takes the baby Jesus in his arms and utters his prayer of thanksgiving (Lk 2:29–32). While the angels announce a Savior for all the people of Israel (Lk 2:10–11), the saintly Simeon praises God for what the birth of Jesus will mean and bring to all the peoples of the earth (Lk 2:30–32).

Then the old prophetess Anna joins the little group gathered around the baby Jesus. In the temple she has spent a lifetime of prayer and fasting. Now she seconds Simeon in thanking God and proclaiming to others that in the person of Jesus the divine deliverer has come (Lk 2:36-38).

What is intriguing about this whole episode in the temple (Lk 2:22-38) is the silence of Mary and Joseph. They say nothing. Only the two old people speak, and they do so inspired prophetically by the Holy Spirit. Simeon and Anna know life's pain and the infirmities of old age. But it is a litany of gratitude, not of grumbling lament, that comes from them. They have waited and waited for the meeting with Jesus. Now they praise God and are ready for the end of their life's pilgrimage.

Some of us may have seen those retirement centers which put a ban on children and dogs. None of that for Simeon and Anna. They are there to welcome the newborn Jesus in the temple precincts. They are ancient and unwell. But they open their arms to the baby, whom they recognize as the deliverer for whom the human race has been waiting.

To make a point, Luke often pairs off people in his gospel. We come across the woman of Zarephath and Naaman the Syrian in chapter 4, Simon the Pharisee and the sinful woman in chapter 7, the older and younger son in chapter 15, the two companions on the Emmaus road in chapter 24. In the second chapter of his infancy narrative, Luke introduces a pair of old people who express their thanks to God and direct others to Jesus.

Remembering Simeon and Anna this Christmas, we would do well to praise the elderly and thank God for the special ways in which they can lead us to Jesus. Their faces also shine in the light that comes from the crib.

The elderly may not always be economically useful. But from a human and Christian point of view, they are immensely valuable. The Church needs her Simeons and Annas. We find the child Jesus in many ways and at different moments—not least in the arms of old people.

Christmas is a feast for all ages: for Chiara and countless other little boys and girls; for young men and women like Giuseppe; for Gino, Fausta and other lovers; for the aging and the elderly; for Sister Angelina and the very old.

This Christmas there will be cribs in the Gesù Nuovo and the other churches of Naples. But the biggest and the best crib you can find is at the center point in the arcade of King Umberto I. Neapolitans of all ages will stop there—to look, comment and pray. Like St. Luke, they know that Christmas is for every-one—a season for all ages.

Chapter Seventeen:
God's Body Language

The centenary of the death of John Henry Newman (1990) was marked in Italy by major congresses in Venice, Bologna, Rome and Leonforte in Sicily. Now a town of around fifteen thousand inhabitants, Leonforte was the scene of Newman's nearly fatal illness in 1833. On his way home to England after his recovery, he wrote "Lead, Kindly Light."

A brief but memorable intervention at this Leonforte symposium raised the question: How did Newman manage to communicate with the local people during his sickness and convalescence? He had little Italian and less Sicilian. The speaker argued that the eyes, the faces and the hands of the locals more than compensated for the lack of any common verbal ground. Generous smiles and gestures overcame all of the difficulties with words. At the end of that intervention I looked around at the crowd of people from Leonforte. "This hall is full of body language," I thought. "These people are still living signs and symbols. When their faces and hands are in full swing, they often symbolize and communicate more than their words ever can."

For the actual anniversary day of Newman's death, 11 August, I was out of Italy, substituting for a priest in one of the tiny Bavarian villages that together make up his parish. The experience of Newman in Leonforte repeated itself again for me—this time in Heldmannsberg. My passable German cannot always break through the country dialect, but the body language of those Bavarians more than made up for any verbal problems.

Just before the Newman anniversary I saw the village burying one of its dead. Everyone was there—in the seventeenth-century church and the adjoining cemetery. With hymns, flowers and tears they said it all. A few days later over a hundred pilgrims came from a neighboring parish six or seven miles away. They moved in procession through the village to the church and celebrated the Feast of the Assumption. Once again the body language of those farming people with their vivid faces came into play. Their singing, vigorous responses, candles, flowers and incense richly expressed their devotion to the Mother of God and their hope to share with her in God's eternal life.

Heldmannsberg and Newman's experience in Leonforte sent me back to the Bible and its living signs and symbols. From the Book of Genesis on, God's communication often takes that form. After the flood, heaven and earth are linked by the sign of the rainbow, which reveals and guarantees God's grace and favor. The rainbow symbolizes God's undying friendship. Like a living thing, a rainbow comes and goes in the sky. The manna in the desert is gathered fresh every morning; it cannot be stored up like dead produce. The classical prophets constantly reach for living signs and symbols to communicate their message from God: an almond tree in blossom, a woman in childbirth, hearts of flesh, people going into exile, potters busy at their work, shepherds with their sheep, vineyards promising a great yield of wine, fountains bubbling with water.

Obviously not all biblical signs and symbols are living. The great sign of God's saving presence, the temple in Jerusalem, was built of stones and other dead materials. But often living symbols predominate: above all, such rich and sacred symbols as blood, which expresses deliverance, purification and pledged friendship. Eventually, even the temple becomes such a symbol when Paul and Peter write of the community of the baptized as God's temple of "living stones" that makes up a "spiritual house."

Whether they are living or dead, signs and symbols are constantly used by God and God's messengers to communicate truth that can illuminate and liberate our human condition. Mere abstract information can seem out of touch and fail to convince. Living symbols invite us to be partners in an ongoing dialogue. They make God present for us in new ways.

Far better than we do, God knows how signs and symbols touch our deepest feelings, stir us to action and lead to heroic commitment.

It comes as no surprise, then, to read the angel's words to the shepherds: "This will be a sign for you; you will find a babe wrapped in swaddling clothes and lying in a manger" (Lk 2:12). The face, mouth, hands and curled-up toes of that tiny baby are God's unique, nonverbal gesture to us. Mary's child is the loving, visible symbol of the invisible God. That baby has made God present for us in a startlingly new way.

We might adapt here the prologue of John's gospel and say: "The Word became body language and dwelt amongst us." What began with body language in the manger at Bethlehem ended with body language when Jesus stretched out his hands and feet to be nailed to the cross.

It takes no great leap of the imagination to read as God's living signs the people who welcome the new-born Jesus. There are the shepherds, roughing it at night and representing the poor of this world who receive God's special blessing. In Bethlehem the shepherds find Mary and Joseph, whose faith and love make them utterly and uniquely open to the divine will. In the temple the aged Simeon and Anna symbolize just what lifelong fidelity to God can mean. The wise men from the East signify the pilgrims of this world, who may travel for years before they find him "who was born king of the Jews" (Mt 2:2).

Intensely symbolic people fill up the Christmas story. No wonder painters, sculptors and musicians have returned to it again and again for themes and inspiration. It comes also as no surprise that Christians have taken a cue from the New Testament texts and added further living signs around the manger: camels, sheep, oxen, dogs and, of course, the Christmas tree. Italians and, above all, the Neapolitans have excelled themselves by introducing persons and animals galore into their Christmas scenes. The instinct is profoundly right and deeply biblical. All those living symbols belong naturally to the story of Christ's birth.

In a year when the world celebrated Newman, I felt deeply grateful to the people of Leonforte and Heldmannsberg. In their different ways those Sicilians and Bavarians showed me one deep reason for the power of the Christmas story. It is through body language that it communicates so much about God and ourselves. The living signs that make up that story draw us into a dialogue that will take us through Christ's life to the final body language of his death and resurrection.

Chapter Eighteen:
A Bloody Christmas

On Christmas Eve 1984 an officer in a training school for Italian railway police shot himself. He was only twenty-nine years of age. In his suicide note he begged his father and two sisters to forgive him for the terrible sorrow he was bringing them. He explained the reason for his act: "For me it is no longer possible to continue to live in this world that is so absurd."

Four years earlier the same young man had been among those who gathered the dead and rescued the wounded after a terrorist bomb killed eighty-five persons and injured hundreds at the Bologna railway station. In December 1984 he rushed with his fellow cadets to the "tunnel of death" on the line between Florence and Bologna. A bomb on a crowded train had left fifteen dead and one hundred and seventeen wounded.

In the darkness the officer worked for hours to save lives and then, in despair, went home to take his own. He was the final victim of what the Italian newspapers called "a bloody Christmas."

There is no disguising the absurd and murderous violence which continues to fill our world. Of course, it all runs against our Western conviction that people are reasonable and that there are solutions to all our problems. Yet it does not stop. Whether it is caused by terrorists, political leaders, drunken football fans or plain criminals, the killing goes on: from Afghanistan to Algeria, from Colombia to Ruanda, from Sicily to Sri Lanka. There are no easy clichés to explain why hatred, greed and fear drive human beings to victimize each other in such brutal ways. It is absurd.

The feasts which follow Christmas make us see something of the same violence. On 26, 28 and 29 December we remember, respectively, a martyred deacon, some massacred children and an archbishop murdered in his own cathedral. The liturgical calendar places the birth of Jesus just before a list of victims. Right from his nativity, Jesus stands in a special solidarity with the losers. Who seems more of a loser than someone who ends like Stephen, the Holy Innocents or Thomas à Becket?

In his suicide note the Italian officer ended by saying to his father and two sisters: "I beg you to continue living life. At bottom it is very beautiful."

Faith in Jesus looks at a human race blasted by the ugliness of savage violence, but adorned forever by Mary's beautiful baby. He came among us not to force anyone into acting reasonably but to invite us all to share his presence and peace. The fact that he ended up crucified between two losers expressed for all time and for all people his human and divine love. Only this love can prove a match for our absurd willingness to kill each other.

THE NEW YEAR

Chapter Nineteen:
Chalking Up a Good Year

Some old customs can still momentarily transfigure our existence and let the eternal shine through. One of these customs needs a little chalk and takes place on or around 6 January, the Feast of the Epiphany.

In parts of Germany and some neighboring European countries a priest will walk through his parish or village, blessing the houses and writing with chalk over the main doorway "1999" and "CMB." The numbers "1999," "2000" or "2001" refer, of course, to the year which is just beginning. The letters "CMB" stand for Caspar, Melchior and Balthasar.

As many readers will have noticed, in its Christmas story Matthew's gospel simply speaks of some "wise men" who come "from the East" and does not give them any names. Matthew does not even say that there were three wise men. But because they offer three gifts (gold, frankincense and myrrh), they were thought to be three in number. It was tradition that gave them the names of Caspar, Melchior and Balthasar.

Chalking up the year "1999" and the letters "CMB" over the entrance to our home is a way of joining ourselves to the wise men from the East. They follow their star, eventually find Jesus and give him their worship. We all wish to follow our star, find Our Lord and worship him.

Some people read a second meaning into the letters "CMB." In the Latin language they could stand for *Christus mansionem benedicat* ("may Christ bless the house"). So writing "CMB" above our doorways means associating ourselves both with the wise men (Caspar, Melchior and Balthasar) and with the newborn child whom they seek and find. May Christ bless all our homes as we begin the year 1999 or 2000 or 2001.

Nowadays in Germany it is not merely priests who bless houses and write over the entrance "CMB" and "1999." There are also the "Star Singers," groups of boys and girls who go around doing just that. These Star Singers move from house to house—singing, chalking up "CMB 1999" and gathering contributions for poor countries. The priests do their chalking and blessing only in Catholic homes. The boys and girls who belong to the Star Singers go everywhere: to Catholic and Protestant homes alike. They bring the blessing of Christ and the example of the wise men to any household that lets them come in—with their songs, their chalk and their collection boxes.

So far I have been reporting what happens nowadays in Germany and some other European countries around the Feast of the Epiphany. Let us go back to the New Testament and Matthew's gospel, where we read the story of the wise men from the East. We pick up their trail when they reach Jerusalem. They have seen a star in the East and have come looking for the new-born king. They are directed to Bethlehem, where, to their intense joy, they find the child Jesus and worship him.

The story of the wise men from the East is a story of those who make the most of the very little they have — just a star that they see once or twice and, at the end, the advice to try Bethlehem. The wise men have come a great distance. They do not know the writings of the prophets and the other inspired Scriptures. But, with the little help they receive, the wise men make it through to Jesus. Finding him fills their hearts with the deepest joy. They have found the baby on whom their lives depend and who deserves nothing less than their adoration.

The wise men make the most of such limited help as they are given. Herod and the religious leaders in Jerusalem could easily find Jesus. They live just a few miles from Bethlehem. They have the sacred Scriptures to direct them in their search. But they squander their chances and fail to discover their newborn King and Lord.

A New Year is beginning. We may feel that, like the wise men, we have been given few chances and little help. Or we may recognize that, like the religious leaders in Jerusalem, God has blessed us with abundant help and many chances. Either way, we can chalk up a good year for the Lord.

May we all let the Star Singers into our homes and listen to their song. For all the readers of this book I pray: May you be like Caspar, Melchior and Balthasar on their pilgrimage. This coming year, as always, may Christ bless your homes.

Chapter Twenty:
New Year's Day and the Naming of Jesus

There are some New Year themes that never die but live on to comfort us year by year. One such is the theme of salvation, as we recall today how Jesus was circumcised and given his name.

In Matthew's gospel an angel of the Lord tells Joseph that Mary "will bear a son, and you shall call his name Jesus, for he will save his people from their sins" (Mt 1:21). Luke has an angel of the Lord telling the shepherds, "to you is born this day in the city of David a Savior, who is Christ the Lord" (Lk 2:11). A few verses later the gospel writer adds: "After eight days had passed, it was time to circumcise the child; and he was called Jesus" (Lk 2:21).

The name *Jesus* means "God saves" or "God is salvation." In this way the very name points Jesus out as the one who is to bring the divine salvation to all men and women. In the New Testament only God and Jesus are called "Savior." This title is never used of others.

At midnight mass every Christmas we hear from the Letter to Titus that "salvation has been brought for the whole human race." We are exhorted to "wait for the blessed hope and the manifestation of the glory of our great God and Savior, Jesus Christ" (Ti 2:11,13).

We are comforted by the Christmas message of salvation. But what are we saved *from?* What are we saved *for?* How can we believe in the salvation offered us as we live out the great tragicomedy that is the human story of each of us?

Where the angel of the Lord promises that Jesus will save his people "from their sins," the Our Father prays more globally, "Deliver us from evil." Certainly we need to be freed from the sins through which we seek our own self-satisfaction and personal benefits to the exclusion of others. But evil goes beyond our individual failure to live a life guided by a true love for God, other persons and ourselves.

We may feel ignored, exploited and at the mercy of some influential majority "out there" in society. Within our family circle we can suffer from grossly inadequate human relationships. Our life can become chillingly dreary. Sickness and the passing of the years leave us gripped at times by a sense of our own vulnerability and mortality.

Besieged by sin and evil in their various forms, we look for someone to free us and bring us what we have been missing. In his second book St. Luke assures his readers that salvation is to be found only in Jesus: "There is salvation in no one else, for there is no other name under heaven given among mortals by which we must be saved" (Acts 4:12). We experience every day our need to be saved. Yet how do we know that salvation is to be found in Jesus—both here and hereafter?

Ultimately it is our ongoing experience that really vindicates Luke's claim. Our relationship with Jesus proves itself in practice. It yields a sense of freedom and peace by delivering us from our burdens of sin and fear.

Others have told us of Jesus. They have taught us to sing hymns to "Christ our loving Savior." They have promised us that through life in the Church he will save us from the numbing routine of evil and give our hearts a quiet happiness. But like the Samaritans we cannot be content to take another's word for all that. We need to experience for ourselves that Jesus "is indeed the Savior of the world" (Jn 4:42).

The New Testament presents our salvation as a real force at work among us and for us. The baby in the manger is already our Savior. Out of his own experience St. Paul can insist: "Now is the day of salvation" (2 Cor 6:2). Nevertheless, the apostle acknowledges that the fullness of salvation has not yet come. The best is yet to be. We live confidently hoping that our relationship with the Son of God will be completed in the life to come (Rom 8:18—25).

Then Jesus will finally and completely save his people, all people, from their sins. Beyond the last shadow of doubt, we will experience and see that Mary's Son is "indeed the Savior of the world." In a relationship with him that will never end, we will have what our hearts really desire and we will know that it is utterly worthwhile.

Chapter Twenty-one:
On Not Following Herod

Back in 1940, when the Second World War had just begun, Dorothy Sayers wrote a series of plays about Jesus for the radio. She called them *The Man Born to Be King*. In the first play Balthazar and the other two wise men visit wicked King Herod. They tell him that they are looking for Jesus, the newborn King of the Jews. Herod is puzzled and says to them: "You speak mysteries. Tell me this: will he be a warrior king?" Balthazar replies: "The greatest of warriors. Yet he shall be called the Prince of Peace. He will be victor and victim in all his wars, and will make his triumph in defeat. And when the wars are over, he will rule his people in love."

Herod, however, is not convinced and tells Balthazar: "You can't rule men by love. When you find your king, tell him so." The old tyrant goes on to justify his position: "Only three things will govern a people—fear and greed and the promise of security. Don't I know it? I've been a stern ruler—dreaded and hated—yet my country is prosperous and her borders at peace." Then Herod adds bitterly: "But wherever I loved, I found treachery— from my wife, children and brother—from all of them, all of them. Love is a traitor. It has betrayed me. It betrays all kings. It will betray your Christ. Give him that message from Herod, King of the Jews."

Rulers down through the ages have practiced Herod's policy and introduced their own variants. Roman emperors provided not only national security but also bread and circuses to keep their subjects under control. Along with food for stomachs and entertainment for the masses, the fear of crucifixion and the threat of lesser punishments persistently played their roles in maintaining Roman law and order. Centuries later the kings of Naples managed their realm through the triple policy of *festa, farina,* and *forca*—that is to say, through festivities, flour and the gallows. Their people were entertained and fed, while the unruly were threatened with harsh penalties that included capital punishment.

Modern states have followed suit with their versions of "bread, circuses and crucifixion." Social welfare programs feed the unemployed. National and international sporting events, media celebrities, soap operas and national lotteries provide the necessary entertainment, the opium that keeps the people happy or at least sleepily distracted. People can sit their lives out in front of a television set. Bigger and bigger jails move criminal offenders off the streets. Soldiers or riot police violently suppress political dissidents. High-tech weapons keep national borders "at peace" while creating catastrophic devastation elsewhere. The cold professionalism of latter-day Roman legions and of those who arm them has fearful results.

Right at the start of the Second World War, Dorothy Sayers warned the masters of the world not to follow the example of Herod and the Caesars. In the long run and often in the short run, the strategy of "bread, circuses and crucifixion" will keep neither the streets nor the borders safe. This policy has an enormous human and economic cost as its price tag. How long can even the most prosperous governments continue to bribe and coerce the electorate? Do the modern equivalents of "fear, greed and the promise of security" create anything else but a moral and religious void that entails a self-destructing loss of values?

The return of Christmas and of the Feast of the Epiphany raises again the question: What forces should rule our individual and national lives? Admittedly, plenty of people are inclined to agree with King Herod that love is a traitor and will betray us all. But we might join Dorothy Sayers in directing their gaze to Bethlehem. The birth of Jesus shows the world a divine love that is stronger than fear, greed and worries about security. If God had been driven by those three forces, Jesus would never have come among us. He would not have been born to a poor mother in a divided and unstable country repeatedly ravaged by war and civil strife.

What Christmas and the Epiphany announce is that true and lasting peace comes through a love that reaches out and is not afraid of becoming vulnerable. Jesus, the Prince of Peace, proclaims genuine love and mutual respect as the true basis of life together. Over and over again since the time of King Herod, societies and their leaders have used greed, fear and frivolous entertainment as their privileged instruments for social control. But in the long run and even in the short run, we see how these instruments prove inadequate politically and fail to satisfy our deepest hungers.

Balthazar's promise provides the only lasting assurance: the Prince of Peace "will rule his people in love." Those who give his love half a chance find the kind of peace that no one can ever take from them, a true security that will never end.

Chapter Twenty-two:
The Three Dark Magi

The German writer Wolfgang Borchert, who died in 1947 at the age of twenty-six, represented a young generation of Europeans who suffered through the Second World War and the years that followed. They hungered for a meaningful existence, for some answer which would overcome the poverty, cold and meaninglessness they experienced. The questions which Borchert raised cannot be limited to the years 1939–47, but have remained to haunt younger and older generations in other ravaged parts of the world.

In "The Three Dark Magi," a story full of shadows and cold, Borchert pictures a young officer who has returned to a bombed-out city from imprisonment in Siberia. Even if the man is angry at his poverty, he still feels the closeness of his newborn child and the human warmth that comes from three injured veterans. They are like a small, comforting light in a freezing, gloomy room. Borchert sees the miracle of Christmas in the sensitive kindness of the three men in shabby uniforms and in the laughter of the child. Light from the oven falls on the sleeping baby to symbolize a new life beginning in the damp night. In the simplest way the kindness of the three veterans expresses the great humanity of God (see Ti 3:4).

He groped his way through the dark suburb. The houses stood, snapped off, against the sky. There was no moon and the pavement was startled by his belated tread. Then he found an old fence. He kicked it with his foot till a rotten lath heaved a sigh and broke off. The wood smelt overripe and sweet. Through the dark suburb he groped his way back. There were no stars.

As he opened the door (it cried as he did so, the door) the pale blue eyes of his wife looked towards him. They came from a tired face. Her breath hung white in the room, it was so cold. He bent his bony knee and broke the wood. The wood sighed. Then there was a sweet and overripe smell all round. He held a piece of the wood under his nose. Smells almost like cake, he laughed softly. Don't, said the eyes of his wife, don't laugh. He's asleep.

The man put the sweet over-ripe wood in the little tin stove. Then it glowed up and cast a handful of warm light through the room. The light fell bright on a tiny round face and paused for a moment. The face was only an hour old, but already it had everything that went with it: ears, nose, mouth and eyes. The eyes must be big, one could see that, although they were shut. But the mouth was open and soft breath came out of it. Nose and ears were red. He's alive, thought the mother. And the little face slept.

There are still some oat-flakes, said the man. Yes, answered the woman, good thing. It's cold. The man took some more of the sweet soft wood. Now she's got her baby and has to freeze, he thought. But he had no one he could hit in the face with his fists because of it. As he opened the door of the stove, another handful of light fell on the sleeping face. The woman said softly: Look, like a halo, do you see? Halo! he thought, and had no one he could hit in the face with his fists.

Then there were some people at the door. We saw the light, they said, from the window. We'd like to sit down for ten minutes. But we have a baby, the man said to them. They then said nothing more, but came on into the room, blowing mist out of their noses and lifting up their feet. We'll be very quiet, they whispered and lifted up their feet. Then the light fell on them.

There were three. In three old uniforms. One had a cardboard box, one a sack. And the third had no hands. Frostbite, he said, and held up the stumps. Then he turned his greatcoat-pocket towards the man. There was tobacco in it and thin paper. They rolled cigarettes. But the woman said: No, the child.

Then the four of them went out of the door and their cigarettes were four specks in the night. One had fat bandaged feet. He took a piece of wood out of his sack. A donkey, he said, it took me seven months to carve it. For the baby. He said that and gave it to the man. What's the matter with your feet? asked the man. Water, said the donkey-carver, from hunger. And the other, the third man? asked the man, as he felt the donkey in the darkness. The third man trembled in his uniform: Oh, nothing, he whispered, it's only

*nerves. One just had too much fear. Then they stubbed out
their cigarettes and went in again.*

*They lifted up their feet and looked at the little sleeping
face. The trembling one took two yellow sweets from his
cardboard box and said: These are for your wife.*

*The woman opened wide her pale blue eyes as she saw
the three dark men bowed over the child. She was fright-
ened. But then the child pushed his legs against her breast
and yelled so heartily that the three dark men lifted up
their feet and crept to the door. Here they nodded again,
then climbed out into the night. The man watched them
go. Peculiar Wise Men, he said to his wife. Then he shut
the door. Fine Wise Men they are, he grumbled, and
looked for the oat-flakes. But he had no face for his fists.*

*But the baby yelled, said the woman, he yelled quite
loud. So they went. Just look how lively he is, she said
proudly. The face opened its mouth and yelled.*

Is he crying? asked the man.

No, I think he's laughing, answered the woman.

*Almost like cake, said the man and sniffed at the wood,
like cake. Quite sweet.*

Today is Christmas, too, said the woman.

*Yes, Christmas, he growled and out of the stove a hand-
ful of light fell bright on the little sleeping face.*

The New Year

God our Father, in a world of darkness and cold people grope for meaning and purpose. Let us offer the sign of our human kindness, which will bring them to your Son, the Light of the world, the One who can cure our anger with his love. Amen.

Sources and Acknowledgments

A number of these pieces have previously appeared (often in a slightly different form) in *America* magazine or the *London Tablet*. The book generally uses the New Revised Standard Version of the Bible; at times the translations are my own. "The Three Dark Magi" by Wolfgang Borchert is reprinted from *The Man Outside,* copyright © 1971 by New Directions Publishing Corp., and is reprinted by permission of New Directions Publishing Corp. and Marion Boyars Publishers Ltd., London.

G. O'C.

Index of Names